THE
MINDS
METAMORPHOSIS

KEITH E. IHOLTS II

Copyright © 2022 by Keith E. Iholts II.

Library of Congress Control Number: 2022910785

HARDBACK: 978-1-957575-85-8
PAPERBACK: 978-1-957575-84-1
EBOOK: 978-1-957575-86-5

Ordering Information:

For orders and inquiries, please contact:
1-888-404-1388
www.goldtouchpress.com
book.orders@goldtouchpress.com

Printed in the United States of America

Contents

ABOUT THE BOOK

This collection of poetry is a story of my life and of changes that have contributed toward what I am today. The poetry ranges from love poems, spiritual aspirations, gothic, abstract and narrative. It is a collection of how an autistic see's the world as if looking out the window at the world yet never able to join. This book contains controversial subjects and profanity as censorship of language goes against free expression. This book contains a variety of poems and short stories that have impacted my life as well as show the particular torment a person lives with having PTSD. I wanted to show the world what looking at the world from my lens's looks like and I am sure there are countless others who prefer a realistic approach as opposed to ignore the hardships this world thrusts on people. A unique perspective of life

I also hope to make aware to people the dangers of religion in how to be controlling. There is a section of poetry from my Christian days that I have kept for the sake of art. From my experiences in living in fear of Christian brimstone preaching which a lot of that fear underlies my earlier work as well as a deep relenting anger at my oppressor that I feared which was religion. Regardless I would love to discuss the role of religion in people's lives and determine how we can live in a society that practices spirituality as opposed to strict rules that are open to interpretation. Traditions is something I have come to hate which can be found in the later portion of the book.

Finally, it is my hopes that my creative writing might inspire further creativity and expression of personal experience. I wish to share my art and have an intellectual experience that opens a person's mind to a bigger universe then they perceived.

ABSTRACT

The first set of poems is my abstract collection. These are some of the works with a twisted reality governed by its own concept of laws. I use abstraction to grasp on concepts we often overlook or consciously subdue. This allows me to reveal the world through the stained glass in order to retrieve a brand-new perspective into life's enigmas. Sometimes it is easier to understand a difficult concept by looking at it from a metamorphic perspective to align its mysteries into a comprehensible whole.

BIRTH OR DEATH?

Trapped, hot, sticky, closure all around me can't break

free, the womb enclosure, breath so sweet yet far from me

Burning air stinging me never, never, never, never,

never

Always, always, always there smiling in the dark bearing

cruel tricks to take

Gasping, gasping, gasping, gasping...

No freedom from the closure that tightens, gripping,

squeezing, tearing, bending, crushing, damn it Let me be

free...

Silence, no more air...no more air...

BREATH

Paths along shadows lined with black roses

I fall...

Holding the hem of breath

A veil of thin dress wafting in the winds of thought

Trimmed icy dressing of time lining frigid dressings of

time

A book holding life's sacred secrets;

The judge,

The jury

I choose.

Whether passing black or pearl determines home

Either place I go you lie in wait to behold

Where I walk or cry depends on where my heart will lie

Gold or fire will embrace my feet that feared night

Smoke and light compete to find what my eyes shall

behold in their sight

Tongue shall meet either bitter or sweet

Visions that haunt my dream are the results of what

father time bleeds

Words are but paint in which we began upon this world

our spirit and light.

Upon the pool of creativity, we reflect unto the world

our sight.

In our madness, we delve deep into creativity.

For that which we can bear no sight the mad dip into
insanity.

For only can we see beyond the veil of reality and
create that which never existed, a new birth in our
world. Only a madman can behold the world to see its
potential.

Only with the touch of insanity can we see beyond the
veil.

Only we can perceive alternate realities.

We share the power of God deep within our hearts.

His presence guides our touch.

INVASION OF THE FLESH EATING ZOMBIES

Amongst the shallows of my wayward heart, I knew of

its Presence

I felt it as a thin pinch on my numb forearm

Like a quickly thrust can on an overloaded shelf

A lacking of certain distinguished revelation

Only the day before I could pick it out from the piles

of hay,

its sharp point gleaming

Now there is only a mass of sharp steel,

peering from the heavyweight of Security

Can't find it now

I suppose it's gone to be replaced by a more necessary

power

Scattered remains of stolen steel

Number them!

That was the Solution

After the insult to authority in the name of hay,

After the countless clones running around borrowing

from themselves,

the trembling giants leaving their dust covered cloud

The asylum of supposed fanatics cried out "I told you so"

Your assumed doctorate in everything means nothing

to me

Accredited researchers and backing your Sources is dead

Oh, I know how far we have come,

this parade of Unquestionable Acceptance

Love Speeches, Imprisoning Haters

Hunt down those who refuse Tolerance

Marching through the fog-kissed streets

In the early hours of morning in your armor protected

jackets

Sure, we have come to the Ultimate Acceptance, while

the rest

of the world burns until You proclaim Victory on the

mounds of flesh You skinned from the

monsters You marked

Ashes smoke as a final blanket

Except the Throne of Power engulfed in the middle of a

sea of fire

MY FATHER AND I

My father and I stood across a chasm of plastic
thought.

A thin veil of translucent wax, thick splattered across.

Never crossing the airy bridge left to rot.

He stood; I walked along the ridge seeking relief from
that damn clock.

I called; he answered with echoed knocks.

I bled, and he would not.

He asked, "Who?" I asked, "What?" He asked, "Why?" I
asked, "Why Not?"

He held his breath, screaming.

I began to run; he only walked a slow trot.

"This way you fool!"

"Who said that?"

"I don't know. Turn off that damn clock."

"I broke the window; I ate your soul."

"I am your mistake; I am your folly!" "My hands are
dirty."

"Well, no wonder! You were cleaning a meat grinder."

"Well, it was full of giblets. Can't you see?"

"First let me deal with that damned slob."

"I don't care what you said about the picture. It just
doesn't fit."

"What is all this amiss?"

"It's your severed heart. Good lunch."

"Eat your lunch; I'm sick of hearing your mouth."

"Forget it, this Never ends."

I crawl down the abyss.

I found his side full of crap.

I went back through the door.

The door is locked.

Wait, this is my spot

So dark

Forget it; I never tried to get it.

TROLL

I went to go see the troll today

He was in the beautiful valley

He must have been in the moors because his feet smelled

like crushed decayed children

I found a trail of dead crows; he must have been hungry

He was tucked neatly away in a corner

I could see his eyes looking right at me

Two stop lights urging me forward

I sought him out to ask some questions

I asked him why he had to eat my arms and legs

Thus, came his reply:

Pulled them right out of their sockets

Took a good chunk out of me

They grew back but just as cheese

I don't know what to do with string cheese arms and

legs of log cheddar

I begged him to eat the cheese but he only seems to like

human flesh; it's so filthy

and that is what he likes

I told him to just eat them; maybe something better

would grow up

Then he took my limbs to beat those damn lemmings

that are always crawling up out of my

coagulated skull

Smashing them into little red bone pies

Laughing like the moronic giant fiend it is

His cloddish self-pleasing grin

I tried to kick him with my lactose intolerant legs

Thus, was his reaction:

He just brushed at his pale skin with a crooked smile

He said "I liked cheese so please partake of such

delicacies" he boasted with pride as he

crammed it down my throat

As he gnawed on my bloody limbs he consumed with glee

Stuffed me like a turkey, but only took the limbs

He ran off with his large blue ass hanging in the wind

to let me know how he got away

I would rip these screwed up limbs of mine off but

they're just too flimsy to remove

I know you have heard this a million times

I don't care that you don't want to hear it

I'm just hungry

DEAD WEIGHT

I dreamed of ivory tonight

I saw the towering picture of his deathly grin obscured

by prison water

He was the prize of captains, the picture of strength

A legend held now by simple wood

How armored tusks could not save your beastly hide

Did the tears of irony seep your heart?

To hold imaginable weight and strength in a hopeless

plunge

I wonder how the mere irony of your humbling capture

add more grief in your death

Did you know of your unstoppable weight until it

caused your sinking?

In death did you finally understand much power you

held?

The power that left you to the depth of watery hell

Did the chains even contribute, but boast of your

execution?

Would it be better to make your home on the seafloor,

rather than parade the weakness that had you held

down?

Even in your ridiculous end you became an idol unto

foolish men

Yet you never knew this coming, you only knew the

chains of strength

WORTHLESS

"Come here and take your clothes off and we'll see"

"It's cold and I don't want to get my feet wet"

"Do it we need to get a good look at you"

"Fine, but don't look at me like that"

"Ok, what we have here is a flaw we need to deal with"

"It's just a freckle. What harm is that?"

"It might grow to be a big freckle that swallows your
body"

"Fine, so what do we do with the freckle?"

"We peel it off slowly"

"Won't that hurt?"

"Not too long it won't, try not to scream while I peel,
it will hurt my ears"

"Just do it quickly, not slow, I don't want to linger
in it"

"There now we have to deal with that gaping wound it
just don't match"

"Wouldn't it have been better had we covered the
freckle?"

"No, you have to be perfect in every way let's remove the
rest of your flesh and use it as a fashionable vest."

"Fine, be careful with it I would like to keep it fresh"

"Look at all that fat it's disgusting"

"Well, you exposed it"

"We need to do something about it, we will pack it up
and sell it to Taco Bell"

"At least we can make some money"

"I'm falling apart help me gather myself"

"No use we need to bottle your organs if they are going
to fall out"

"Will it be a little hard to live without my heart?"

"Forget that, you don't need one, you will be fine now
we can decorate the house"

"You are getting blood all over the place stop bleeding"

"I can't I don't have any skin remember?"

"Looks like we need to hold your blood in pitcher's
great drink for later"

"Just make sure you remember to refrigerate it I hate
hot blood"

"Your muscles are so flimsy we will take them and make a
rubber suit"

"Isn't it at least better to have some muscle then none?"

"Do you want to be perfect or not?"

"Be sure to wrap them in plastic to keep the suit clean"

"Let's put these bones to use"

"What is wrong with my bones?"

"They are so... bland... we can make a house of bones"

"Be sure to use plenty of mortar to keep them together"

"What is that hovering about?"

"That's my soul."

"What good is that for? Can we sell it?"

"No not really it's not important at all"

A DATE WITH DEATH

I saw death, she was lovely.

She held a baby in her arms to nurse him.

Isn't that sweet?

I saw how she cradled him singing such gentle songs of
old age.

He drank her age and so quickly.

He fell asleep with wonderful wrinkles all over his face.

She then kissed him as she began to eat.

Such a delicious dinner she ate.

She invited another who liked to play.

He played games with her all the time.

He liked to follow her and run away.

She is so nice how she let him always get away.

He loved to boast of his playful ways.

This bothered her so she decided he should go away.

When she finally caught him, boy did he get a surprise!

He was delicious, I'm sure, with his tender thighs.

I JUST DON'T KNOW

I find myself trapped in this cage of writer's block, of
life with a metronome clock lock.
Forced to gaze upon the zombie TV,
I find myself watching that perilous foaming sea of
expression and ideas dissipate into a speechless mass upon
the empty beach sand without grain or texture feeling
as a fake plaster beneath my feet.
Viewing the steps from times past all seems confusion
and mess as I recall chasing ghosts of promises to find
myself dissipate into the fog of deceit.
I finally come to that tombstone of that broken mirror.
I behold a ghost that holds his heart in high esteem
high above embracing its beautiful touch.
It's haunting comes from time to time the stench of
unforgiving love.
My only company is that memory of those long walks by
the sea with my only true love.
The invincible arms that held me tight in that dark
cellar of solitude.
Trapped within this room I stare at that blinking screen
that absorbs these memories.
Absorbed and stolen I am nearly complete to enter this
world of zombies.
Another product of society's manufacturing plants.

Perchance I find some peace in this last resort of poetry.

Perchance I have found the key to these empty dreams.

THE DARK CORNER

I walk upon this dream of light a loose feather in great

flight

Cast into the dark corner, I hide forever

Alone, forsaken, I cry out in anguish alone in this

bright room from a dark corner

Aloft comes a brilliant light, a woman clothed with

the sun upon her hair and the moon under her feet

Her face so pure and white it blends in with the sky of

light

Hair as the sun flowing up within the holy air

Long dark eyelashes that beckon me to her grasp, to feel

her warm touch that comforts my screaming soul

Her siren call tells me to be of comfort and to hold

onto love

Her presence and touch offer relief, yet I resist with

such a fight

Her eyes dark as jasper take me in and try to hold me

down to her ways

I cannot hold onto such a hope lest the pain be made

too great

My desire grows deeper than the crystal seas of

forgotten tears that shed from shattered hearts

I cannot run I am trapped by her stare, yet this must be

an illusion to draw me near

Near to that dark hole of broken dreams

Where men lie dead from hopes shattered on the rocks

of despair

I cry out to feel her comfort, leave me be in my dark

despair

I cannot trust this feeling of warmth and love

The lie that holds her hair flowing as snakes, I must

not yield lest she consume me

I feel for an escape and flee her plea for this shattered

dream that I no longer can grasp onto

I killed that creature in me that held so dearly to this

foolish aspiration with great care

He was weak and only suffered the poisons of the

emerald dream

I slew him with no content least his weak stare brings

me to her control

A control of chains who does not exist holding me in a

prison with no walls

It is a tragedy to be trapped within an illusion

I drew out my dark dagger of contempt of this day and

age

I lunged for her throat lest she slay me first

Time slowed and I was brought down to the floor just

for her to hold me in her soft arms again

I cannot move and the dagger dissipates in the thin

cold air

Her words so soothing put me in this sleep

I want to trust, yet it is a great fear so I began to

thrust

Mothering she smoothed my hair and feels my face

How long shall you run from me?

How long shall you fear my touch?

How is it you think you may escape my comforting song?

You are but one of many to fall into my power

Her touch that poised above me birthed in me the hated

creature that is desire

The blood of the creature named Desire cries from the

earth and refuses silence lest hate suffocate it from

bitter rage

I cannot escape his demands and he shall sate his thirst

or burn with hellish fires

I must learn to live with such desire for I cannot simply

kill him for he is eternal

As I ponder these bitter wars within, a sight once again

draws my eyes afield

That which yearns for my attention draws me near as

the siren, my heart wanders astray

She speaks again to me in hushed whispers as velvet

curtain's part for our communion

Come to me and let me do my work

Do not try to run anymore nor give into unreasonable

demands

Silence him with sweet promise of that protection he so

craves

That passion should not be bled but fed till the release

that shall heal all the dark wounds and shadows

The dark sands of time whose grains of sand embed

deep within my flesh shall be purged and cleansed and

strengthened shall she lend to protect me from my

hatred and dark desires

Love speaks with tender tones to hold hope once again

and be remade anew

Her voice shatters the veils of shadows that sought to

consume

"Let not evil grow in triumph over your past wounds

that grow deep every waking hour.

The fire that burns deeper than the darkest seas cannot

be quenched for it is God's flame buried within your

broken frame.

Be of a patient heart and do not defame my holy name.

I have looked upon this planet and foreseen the joining

of all.

I have placed the flame within your heart that my job

should not fail and all shall know me as the comforter

of the dark world in which those false bearers of my

name shall bring destruction to their captives.

I am not your enemy but shall free you from that dark

corner."

THE BOX

There is a box in a corner covered in cobwebs

It has one hinge ripped apart and the lock is busted

An empty symbol of what was robbed

Blood stains and grime spot, it's scarred edges

Holes that stare as soulless eyes

Missing gems looted long ago it has no appeal

A cold bitter mist enfolds the box hiding its forgotten

bliss

An odor of dampness wafts from the cracks in its walls

It lies there forever in the corner

The owner of the box weeps in another corner

He casts longing puppy dog eyes upon the box, tortured

by his desire

On a pedestal upon 12 stone steps surrounded by a dark

river sits another box

Veins of gold curve in pattern, gems inlaid deep within

A light pours upon its lid

Cherubim touch wings at the tips to hide the glory of

what's within

Warmth that heals the cold hard wind of her bite

illumes within the man's sight

Velvet lining to cushion its soft insides it hides the key

to that which lies beyond the walnut door

A soft welcoming fragrance wafts above, calling

the timid man away from his spot arising above the
shadowed corner crawling to desire who waits up the
stairs
Slowly he treads up the stairs across stony rubble and
through thick cobwebs that bind his hair
Staring across the dank river that surrounds his prize,
he quivers at such a sight
With a shudder of anticipation, he plunges in without
thought to seek out his prize
Arising from the murky depths of the river that divides,
he steps forth dripping of the river's heavy burden
He begins to climb up the steep slope that bears his prize
A lengthy climb he trudged up to that prize,
standing tall he reaches out, his grasp slowly with
steady, retracing hands that begin to fold back
His smile fading into a fearful snarl with clenched eyes
shut he reaches out to open what he fears above all, the
emotions he held with contempt draw his heart nigh to
the prize he fled so long ago.
Slowing opening the box with shut eyes, grimacing
before beholding such a sight
One eye after another creeping open like an old oak
door to behold the prize
One by one they open wide in wild fear with a screaming
terror deep within, the memories tearing back his
resolve and shattering his strength

Slamming it shut he almost hears a giggle dashing

down the flight of stairs.

Wildly dashing down the stairs, falling fast he

crashing into the riverbank.

Jumping down into the river screaming madly for cover

he scurries across the rubble covered in cuts and bruises

Hunched in a ball in the corner staring deeply at the

box in the corner

The image sharp of the dark master

I have your key but does it matter, no lock, one hinge

two gaping holes within

I can take what I want without such a bother and leave

it to others for further plunder

A smile as wicked as the snake consumes his darkened

shrouded face

Echoing the words in the wind, it's the bitter chill

that has no end

WILLING CAPTIVITY

Wall-less prison, bar less captivity, hold me tight to madness and insanity. My desired chains and massive weights, the love I seek shall hold me away from thee. Into the windows that sold its member to the flashing screen that promised sweet ecstasy far from hell's burning hole has delivered me to such folly that sold me to ignorance's prison. My only crime is naught but complacency. Love of hate bears distraction in the fog of war. I am the distraught millions that once held tyrannies bane, I am the hand that once held justices hammer that wrought liberties mighty bells. The masses that once loved freedom but sold her as a trinket for show comfort and empty laughter. What was grand has become a shadow trapped in sinking sand. What once looked to heaven to guide abandoned clean sight to artificial light. What held a lamp to darkened paths now walks willingly to captive halls for the oppressed mass. That our hearts shrink to fill the stomachs of the few. With no hope beyond this rock, the Empty priests that bear lies of only an empty void rob reason and truth a chance to declare, freedom lives and breathes to bring us home once again.

BY GOD, THE SANDMAN QUIT AGAIN

No sand to grace my eyes tonight, no granted passage
to rest in a world of unrealities. Trapped in a plane
of pale black clenched with stubborn eyes demanding
entry. Not even a no from beyond the gates but an
echoed plea from stuttered lips. Follow along the
gates to peer deep across the landfill. The gathered
trash of dreams of others. Some horrors that shy
the heart from a private hell, others of grand design
the creators of others hell, some of the heroic deeds
echoed from a horrendous cheer, others of a simple
glass of lemonade on a green grass lawn on a perfect
day. I walk along an endless fence with none of my own
to hold on but a vale of black curtains that dare me
to cross over. Guessing of the wonders beyond of what
hearts transpire within who knows if it's any more than
a thick fog with simple wishes to hold on. No more do I
fly along the sky to be among an ocean of stars. Instead
of swimming along a black sea with no end at all.

WANT TO BE FREE

I'm a lone man on a lone road sailing the skies on a
Following where the sea may breathe and the land is
free chains are a myth to our feet with no desire to
leave, I just want to be free.
Taken by the winds wherever they lead, take me on a
journey to find where minds sail along golden leaves,
just break me free where no laws abide with hate and we
are truly redeemed, take me to that forbidden dream.
Following where the sea may breathe and the land is
free chains are a myth to our feet with no desire to
leave, I just want to be free.
Hello, eagle my brother take me by your wings to soar
among eternal stars, tear drop skies of sweet release a
song from my lips the sweet nectar of lovely hope among
the ocean of blessed points of light burning my soul.
Following where the sea may breathe and the land is
free, chains are a myth to our feet with no desire to
leave, I just want to be free.

GOTHIC POETRY

This part of my poetry is an expression of pain and alleviating pent-up emotions about the world in which I often felt I had no control. I must warn there is some profanity in some of them. It is the age-old question about rather we really have control over our lives or are victim to fate. It is all metaphorical of course and please do not take into any of this poetry as literal as it is not intended to be literal. There is some rather violent and gory imagery placed in some of these poems and is meant to represent the chaotic, violent rage that builds up in us all. It is the ID that lies within us seeking to devour us and leave only a husk of what we once were. It is the primal nature that lies in wait in the depths of our own personal hell. This portion of poetry is to recognize that part of us as a means to understand the evil within us but without succumbing to its seductive nature. To hold it in is only to garner an even greater explosive force in the end yet it is a dangerous study to understand our dark side. "If you gaze into the abyss, the abyss gazes into you". - Friedrich Nietzsche

RED INK

These scars are just the marks from where I drew the
ink. To write upon the darkest wall painted with human
taint. The gradual shade that bleeds in thin air thick
with must. I walk the shadow's path yet without coming
to the end that I forever chase till the light turn the
other way and I must turn around and forever chase
anew. Where the beating heart does flow my footsteps
follow to the point of finding the river shallow and
sand does quench my throat. Is the river a dream? Is
mine quest the fool's errand? I found a key with no
lock least rust made her expire. Mine treasure the
search yet more like the fool's punishment. The rose
mural my mockery, a black rose my signature on an empty
grave where alone I shall forever remain. I held the
rain drops from my broken windows where my secrets
lay hid in their ruins. What stung with salt now is a
sweet life that runs down my scars, my ink and farewell
forever.

PIN CUSHION

If you think I am emotionally immature let me tell you
a story to make it clear. There once was a boy alone
and full of fear. His eccentric difference cut him off
so none could be near. Mocked and broken, so few he
held dear. Lies and scorn awaited him where learning
could never quite take hold except hate, his only escape
from the tyranny. His home from whence his escape
could be so near was devastated by educational tears.
Never a night to hold close a place to heal but see the
masquerade of rage displayed every year. Never the one
held but leaned upon by those who created him to let
out the pain created by existence that buried him in
shame. For every pin, a name appeared to remind him
of life's cruel game of purpose, he never could escape.
Anger, hate, rage, guilt, sorrow, shame, a place to hold
tears. Each a pin pricked close to a heart that could
not contain another needle for every spot was claimed.
Never one to unleash his agony, forever made to hold
the weight made by a forgery of love that forever
seared. No answers, only confusion to never know what
to say but silently absolve sins he never understood but
held to with bitter grudges he sought to escape. The
fury of the nights, he held the lock with no keys where
skill could not solve the problems that were laid before

his feet. Never a time to grow and develop, only time to weep in silent graves. I never know what happened to this boy left to the shades. Long ago was his death where the body never decayed. Only a fragile imprint of his soul burned into that dark wall. A shadow trapped in tormented pose, a shapeless shadow is all that remains to this day. To understand these trials is to understand dead youth left to decay. I am not here because I was never allowed to be born in my early years. I am not this boy, this is not my story. This is only a reflection of what stares from the mirror. I am not he...I am not he...I am not he... I am simply not there.

RESTING PLACE

I must aspire to the fields of green where my heart came to grieve. The jotted landscape where memories held free does create the storm within me. I hold a candle in these cold winds where bones creek old. Where the whispers of ancient echoes consume my every thought. The spirits do wave in the wind, such sweet melodies adrift in the air. My mortality a looming expression, a wretched grin. The sight of life's thin strain stretched to the brim. My sullen cries dying on short breaths within.

HELL EYES

I find no end to this misery. This pain in my heart bears cruel remarks. I think of relief every day and I look up to empty skies. No freedom from this agony that tears at my soul. I am cursed but for what reason, I am not told. I bear my tortured eyes in question to the God of all our lives. How long shall I endure this tortured mind? I am exhausted as sleep brings on silken strands the nightmares that plague my mind. I feel alone and cold with no relief. I am taunted by tainted history. God, where are you in this hell. Am I imprisoned to this place from former death? Is this reality of constant threats of eternity that eats me alive with fear punishment for a time my soul cannot place? I ache in every bone and muscle for release and there is no peace... no peace...no peace...not even in sleep.

MARCH OF THE HUSK

I left my body in a room where the death took my soul yet denied my body to leave this world. Empty I walk the shadowed street where every shade is a monster to my past. I cannot see beyond the blood-stained horizon but the damnation of my shell roams the empty streets. The grime of my story reveals the agony in search of sustenance to again make me whole. Never satisfied from the hunger and thirst for what made me human but a cycle of rage that sets the mind on fire with the devil's subtle touch. I seek to find the answers life denied me but only find questions to heap on. A sound, a smell, a slight change in the environment and I follow the trail. Never knowing why but have no other sensation to draw me but what surrounds me is my compass. My map just so I can have an excuse to move and no longer slumber in the drought of death. This is my existence, this is my hell when all original thought is dictated by the world all around. Welcome to the artists hell.

BRANDED

Your eyes are darkened to the eyes of another you never meet. Your heart does not carry the wound so deep you left in me. Should I find an oasis from your heartless touch what cause to lead you to my defilement your memory severed to the rotting touch of alcohols wiles? What insanity birthed in that warped mind to leave me in hateful shame. How can you forgive a demon that crushed innocence I shall never see? Not until the demon shall once again smirk at me. An injustice that drives me to madness in this twisted reality. Bathed in blood so callously spilled in self-hate. I cannot cover sin that is not mine nor has heavenly purity. I burn in confusion where my heart seeks love it can never understand. An echo on the wind bearing tragedy.

No ears to hear or a soul that understands how to balance another's sin with a secret. I took my promise to the razor and in blood, I marked my vow that my soul shame remains in hell lest I offend my heavenly father with perversions foul smell. I sought the shadows that my wicked life spares me from my heavenly father's sight. In a sick rage did I scar my flesh with blade or knife. I find solace in my shed blood tasting sweet with sin and bile to the stomach in self-inflicted cannibalism. Such hot-sweet flavor coating my throat to soothe the guilt branded with a touch and searing hot eternal

with blighted words that killed the last innocence

in me. Why is it sin to take pleasure in deaths most

subtle touch? Just a moment to feel her fingers across a

receding blush. To know the shame of a dishonest night.

I write my stories in shallow wounds that run deep.

I can't determine what is sanity, only that long ago

my mind was lost. I lie hear a testimony to the broken.

Shall we unite in a mass of self-destructive fights? Let

our sorrows bleed out into the night. Satan's call a

cruel mockery that stirs my soul with unearthly fright.

He beckons revenge from dark curled lips spilling lies

yet I cannot break away from that goat's willy eyes. I

preach no submission to the lord of death, destruction,

and hellfire but to flee his wicked delights. His only

cause is unjust revenge against the holy lord of Godly

might. How my heart does sing to hear his loving words

but my soul must be quite the fright. Be warned of my

tale of the godless plight and sing to the lord of the

righteous least your spirit eternally expires. God save

me from me. The demon that held the filth of a child's

night infects my soul with heavy guilt that kills on

sight.

THE HARVEST

I left my body in a room where the death took my soul yet denied my body to leave this world. Empty I walk the shadowed street where every shade is a monster to my past. I cannot see beyond the blood-stained horizon but the damnation of my shell roams the empty streets.

The grime of my story reveals the agony in search of sustenance to again make me whole. Never satisfied from the hunger and thirst for what made me human but a cycle of rage that sets the mind on fire with the devil's subtle touch. I seek to find the answers life denied me but only find questions to heap on. A sound, a smell, a slight change in the environment and I follow the trail. Never knowing why but have no other sensation to draw me but what surrounds me is my compass. My map just so I can have an excuse to move and no longer slumber in the drought of death. This is my existence, this is my hell when all original thought is dictated by the world all around. Welcome to the artists hell.

GENERATIONAL DECAY

My generation was ruined by the pretentious, self-absorbed narcissists that brainwashed us into believing their hypocritical, plastic society that put us in. We were subjected to a simple caste system that turned us into cattle to be a generic herd. They chimed in their obsession with a war on drugs that made them fat off of the American pie diet that was our dignity. Categorized and self-fulfilled prophecies of failure and self-denial. A herd of customer service representatives nothing short of slaves. We take in all the self-entitled, pig faced the public that treats us like machines that don't process exactly to their orders. We bear the shame of low-income forced into overpriced coffins of homes forever trapped in debt force fed by the tube of bureaucracy. Rent and down payments to barley succumb to a life of poverty. Trapped in wretched work cubicles, our freedom an illusion as we shamble our way to our work grounds. A generic brand of people, plastic wrapped into "normal" packaging. Selling to us, obsessions that become our idols and gods. The thrill of individuality trampled by normalcy. The insane bearing relevance to what is real but has been branded mad. Shuffle us into the theater of life through reality TV tearing at our very privacy that is continually monitored by the perverts of government. A cancer of liberty and freedom eating away at our souls leaving us into color coded montages of our progression as a species that fosters a rebellious spirit of youth to create their own mark on history. As of committing graffiti on the fabric of time. We seek diversity and yet find ourselves forever brought to the comfort of human company. Are we all individuals acting out or are we one giant individual forged into this mockery of unity? How can we call ourselves a unity of our own being when we dress as one another, we copy trends and sayings that flood our language? The internet a mass of various cultures, beliefs and unspoken rage at one another fills my head with noise and I can no longer hear what I am saying. I am uncertain as to what I am speaking as I can no longer hear my own voice. Never cut off from sound until this maddening silence followed by the wails of unspoken secrets gilded with human misery. I no longer understand my own words for I have become deaf to the noise of modern society. Complications and bureaucracy the rule of the land with convoluted laws to allow civilian abduction for corporate profit. I fear the shadows of this gentle land. Where monsters hide and the devils in humanity seek the flesh to sate their hellish needs. I see the world from behind closed curtains. Translucent to the point where insanity has become my reality. I can just make out the world before me but I never recognize it. It's forever changing colors and background. What I remember yesterday is ancient history and what is today ages quickly in this monotonous cycle of human error. Where profit was never enough another scandal that is invisible to the blind would surface in the call and outcry at imagined enemies. Our police often more of a predator than the protector, our leader's mob bosses with no limit to their evil. No sanctuary in this land that mocks peace and unity. It is full of predators whose gluttonous greed knows no end. Their separation from reality and the lower classes driving them into a state of schizophrenic denial. Their world full of rainbows and gold pots void them of the soul that tethered them to earth. Their gaze empty of any compassion as they unveil themselves as gods. Our culture is nothing more than a pagan cult seeking gods of pleasure. So desperate to escape our realities, we revel in false existence. Rather video games, books, TV, Movies, food, drugs or whatever indulgence you crave we are all addicts trying to escape a dismal existence and when we turn our backs on the reality we let the world fall back into the hands of evil. We let the tyrants, thieves, and crooks rise from the bile of human inadequacy to consume us as an undead horde and can never sate their carnal pleasures. Our false realities that fuel this disease oligarchy infuse them with their own false reality of godhood. Where their fellow man is but a stepping stone to their own indulgences. Our entire society is founded on obtaining the perfect reality so we can escape the one we have abandoned. We bring about our own destruction when we refuse to face the errors of human behavior. We let the garbage heap about us and the insects come to devour. When will we wake from these realities and start to make our own reality free from the monsters of society that lurk in the shadows preying on the weak? The only question I have to ask now is...Is it too late?

ECHO

My eyes are shut, yet I am awake

A distant rumble

Screaming, fighting, hating, arguing, insulting,

rejecting, filthy, vengeful

A subtle silence

Grief, death, pain, hate, anger, revenge, unforgiving,

worthless, dirty

When will I wake up

GRAVEYARD

To be a great writer the cost is countless wounds and
scars
Breaks into his heart, yet it will never mend and golden
treasures he shall discover
Liquefying himself on pages as hot molten lava or cool
spring waters inscribing as snakes the maddened passion
of a flurry of words of what he was, is, and is to become
Be it light or dark choice one, to mix is the oil and
water the vomit of God
Rather his words dug from graves or passion borrowed
it is the robbing of a dead man's treasure
Yet as any morbid writer would strive to wear a dead
man's jewels and crowns
Ring of death encircled about your scrawny finger
Heavy crown to cast your eyes on the rigid ground
A knight of poetic death inscribing on his resting place
Six feet from success the grand writings his marker
shall possess
Price tag of great art is the inscription upon his
tombstone that sings his lively tunes
Yet the tales always shall lead back to death
Resting place another tomb of forgotten treasure

THE GREAT FREAK SHOW

I cannot hold this which beat within the depths of the

frozen cold heart.

The beating of a dead man's wishes in which I have not

yet escaped the dark.

The world in which my soul sings is sullen to the roots

of where dead hearts continue to beat,

Musical wonders that amaze the world to how the

dead make music while so weak.

Pounding globs of molten candy down their scar

scratched throats as they watch us drown in such

sorrows,

Holding tickets to show their right to bear their eyes

down on another,

Freaks to be shown among the world's glamorous eyes,

why do we bother.

To hold these tears that bleed from such enormous

gaps,

Such pious dreams, now only the broken-toothed stones

that line our hearts, earthly tombs...

Do the inscriptions of poured soul on forgotten leaves,

brown and old redeem,

or does the holding cell of our souls bear our pain

forever past the black curtains that beam,

With utter darkness all about our chains being the

fame in which our lives paid with such scars,

scars that mark our hate, our anger, our most

forbidden fate, how cruel that such gifts, no bars

that hold us with a price that inflames the soul that

many for miles around about may see us burn.

Burn with such bright colors of agony and disbelief yet

even such crowds wish for their turn,

To amaze, to bring such delight in countless millions

that bear witness our shame,

to bring about an end to their day by the witness of

countless lives that these pages did claim.

Such agony to know that such beauty has a cost, this

endless cycle of human misery,

yet such a delight to witness and desire, a trap that

only such fools may require.

Our ink lies not in black but is the blood we shed that

you may relieve desires,

desires to see spectacle from our written tales and

poetic lingo, a costly price, I am no liar.

Go ask God of such tears collected, whisk amongst the

sea of our collected shame,

Only he understands us, that bearer of all of our cries,

he redeems our souls made lame.

EYES

Look into my eyes, beyond the darkened rimmed windows

to see my dread

Held in contempt by chains, bearing guilty weight held

to a wall of isolated worlds of decay.

See the hopeless state I lay in filth eating my wage

To merge with hate such crimes giving birth to

endless lies

Here I stay within a state of darkened wait for some

light to burn out my eyes

From the pale sunken holes streams of blood pouring

forth from the sockets an endless river carrying empty

hopes and dreams

To release the flow of venomous rage upon my

forsaken ways

From the punctured holes in my soul, see the drain

that's left me so old

Stench of flesh, stench of foolish ways led back to

indulge in my frivolous ways

Left to feast on my folly to drink of ignorant ways

In my stony womb of hell hidden from sight and grace

LONELINESS

Loneliness is my best friend

He is the only friend I know

He sticks to me in my darkest hour

He is with me when no one's there for me

He walks with me in the empty streets

He carries me in my dreams

He flees after me with every passing moment

He consumes my every thought

He stalks me every day

He sings to me in the dark silent night

He is there when I am in pain

He holds me when I cry

He is what I feel day by day

He sleeps beside me at night

He teaches me what I am supposed to know

He is all that I know and obey

He discovered me in my infancy

He was born by my side

He will be there when I die

Who sticks to my side better than loneliness?

Yes, loneliness is my best friend

CLEAN LIVING

I hang my head in shame, I picture on a blood painted wall

Steam rising from the moment of impure pleasure

Burning off the pain that stretches deep roots to the

cracked heart

Tears could not come so they opened through

another way

The paint that decorates is the sorrow leaked from

unseen eyes

Strings as the laughter my heart hears that mocks its beat

Faces melt like burning wax on fresh wounds

My only mirror a cold steel knife, staring back at me

What looks back is colder, crueler and full of

unrelenting anger

Knocking on death's door pleading mercy, the knife,

the key, yet so hard to turn

Beckoning echoes from dark forgotten chambers beg

it on

Thinly sliced smiles a drawing of my criminal but he is

never caught...

He always gets away, his partner only left as the shade

My hand cannot grasp what memory fades as the dry

sand

All's that's left is intoxication footprints

A path on an endless shore... bearing only my slow

dragged path along

Crawling back to the dark cave where I may lie to perish

with my pain

No matter how I plead I cannot receive peace... I am

left in an early grave

Death, I cried, to cover her sweet dirt over my

wounded heart

My tombstone, a black rose the night envies for her

luster

Plucked are my eyes, robbed like a home in the night,

broken windows left to stare

Glass shattered in cut to the marrow abandoned as the

long-forgotten house

Can anyone hear the cries in the dark, amongst the

moon's vengeful shadowed light

My tears as the river of Styx to carry the dead to their

eternal homes

Hell could not burn from my flesh the horrors of what

flesh had witnessed that night

In time I shall know this place where there is never

ending cleansing pain

Though I scrub, though I burn, nothing shall relieve

the untold filth I carry

Alone I cry into the empty sky, where is my light, my

hope when my world has fallen apart

What was my crime but the first cry telling the world I

exist?

Was it their cruel sneers and accusations that held me

down to punish me for claiming life?

I am weary of this endless war... I want to be free from

these unjust chains

Release me I plead but I only hear their scorn

Whom to accuse of this world's troubles... but a mistake,

a mark upon the world's pretty face

It is I whom shall be the world's trophy of secret

shame... placed upon a mantle of lost dreams

Why me? Why me? Why me? I cannot ask enough and

receive no answer to drive my heart to rest.

FINAL RESTING PLACE

Death came from above with a thundering thud
With its chill came its breathtaking my resolve with
her kiss
Took me as the child in a ride above such fires, I left
the world above to sing in her choir
Dressed amongst the chains that rattle she ever did
know how to cuddle
Up against such cold breasts nurtured me I was left in
such ambiguity
What purpose one could hold against mine eternal soul
Rose colored lips turned black as night, her soothing
song is my love life
Grayest eyes pierce my heart, her empty stare is my future
Frailest hair mingled as salt and pepper, this is my silent
drift upon Styx
Buried me six feet, while I continued to breath
Now I wait in solitude for the haunting air to expire
I do not bother to sigh or scream for the echoes will
shatter my already tattered dreams
Sleep I must... never shall my eyes part the laden dust
Disturb not in my rescue... for out of death's grip takes
me from my refuge
Thudding feet only disrupt the soothing drumbeat that
tells me I am not yet dead
Leave me, my tomb and stone be as I rest in peace

THE UNWANTED

It starts with a heated moment of passion's fire

Burning through what would have been a well-wrought

home

Till the day the seed is found growing as the result of

sin

Developing nine months to wake in punishment he will

take

To burn amongst unwanted weeds, an unwanted

connecting chain

The tears he sheds from his birth start the river of

endless pain

Yes, we are the unwanted. The forsaken and afraid

Just a bunch of fucking mistakes to burn on your

mantle of shame

First day of school to march amongst uncaring faces

Misunderstood and hated we held to our own alone

and in pain

Unseen tears birthed from those who accused us of

misunderstood ways

Struggling to fit in a leave it to beaver world with a

dysfunctional reality

Teacher don't care nor try to understand just move

him in with all the other damn problems

Label him a fool and a failure that will be his name, we

don't have time to care for that mistake

Yes, we are the unwanted. The forsaken and afraid

Just a bunch of fucking mistakes to burn on your

mantle of shame

Schools long and gone the drugs can't seem to relieve,

adult my ass I could care less

Take your leadership and responsibility leave it to beaver

we don't give a fuck anyways

Take your dreams and let us be, under a black cloak of

unforgiving misery

Take it all I don't care anymore, blame me for your one

sad thought and cast me away

Take your joy, take your fucking fake ass made up

happiness and shove it up your tight closed ass

Take my pain, take my burden with me regards to your

long dead mother, then come and say your shit

Yes, we are the unwanted, the forsaken and afraid

Just a bunch of fucking mistakes to burn on your

mantle of shame

I'm not a fucking failure just a man who bears a heavy

burden

I'm not a fucking loser, just a man that's been cheated

of fair game

I'm not a fucking asshole, just a man who's suffered a

bunch of idiot's games

I'm not a fucking nobody, just a man who blends into

your hypocritical background

I'm not a fucking troublemaker, just a man who shows

your face in a broken mirror

I'm not a fucking mistake, just a man who was born from

someone's thoughtless fuckup

No, we are not the unwanted, the forsaken and afraid

No, we are not a bunch of fucking mistakes to burn on

your mantle of shame

We are your judges you fucking pricks who think to

judge us

With what judgment you proclaim shall be judged on

you

We are the bearers of man's dumb ass mistakes and we

learn from the wisdom of pain

So, fucking take your happy go ass life and shove it

cause you're a product of hell and you know it

MIRROR

Red streaks from suppressed pain painting the reflected

surface of their cause

Teardrop paths that lead to down the false yellow brick

road where the prison has begun

Ended life only a step away from the edge of miseries

place

The windows gleam with its yearning the light of relief

so close yet so far away

Hopeless cries to a hopeless void with no answers in

turn

Heartless fate to an ending world where hell awaits

Who shall pay for the shiny streaks that reveal man's

ways

That which looks back demands the life force that

stole from him any joy

What was sacrifice for another has become demand to

repay the favors of man's reward

That which lurks within is now without and demands

satisfaction from his guests

Guests who have determined that they shall remain

within his world shall impart the art of their being

upon the nail-streaked wall

Evidence of their passing shall endure for centuries

told

Who will part on this place that no one dared to go

and now it has become their resting ground

Fate is the investments of which was put in an empty

soul

Partake of your fortune let the moon glow full with

the vengeance of witnessing their crime

Rivers are forever and untold containing crimes

Nothing left within that blank face but a corpse of

eternal hate

Eat of the results you birthed in the nightmares you

raised

A prison that held that person is now the

interrogation of regaining lost innocence

Reader beware...the abyss that stares

JUDGMENT

Condemners of life, in tune with the melodies of hate

Slain innocent blood cries from the desecrated graves

Risen amongst societies ashes, screams are the lullaby of

death's beckoning

How we shall slay in drunken rage the thirst for the

blood of those whom we pleaded

From these unholy grounds shall the dead take our

cross of shame to nail our accusers to their fate

Drown in our tears O wicked beasts, those small beads

God held so dearly

Filth is our coats to torment us with bearing witness

to the holy judge

High above holding the broken infant we faint as

promised ecstasy fills out deprived lungs

Fire, blood, and death come O ye rains of our eternal

visions

Let them see the world promised in our youth to bear

upon them our gravestones

Feel the bitter weight that fury has burned on our

broken backs

Can you who feel the sting of past feel better relief

than be burdened with their horrid screams

Silence now amongst the dried reeds, the swamp of our

lodgings unfamiliar to our touch

So long we logged amongst young rot

Sleep overtakes the restless souls

No more

DEATH IS A STALKER

Death came upon in swift rape as a robbed dark figure

holding back her face behind a black veil promising

mystery

She lifted me upon her high and held me in her arms as a

suckling babe

Pushed upon a wrinkled nipple to drink from her

venomous age

Long spidery fingers that glide across my soft face

wrinkles creasing

Holding me in her tempt singing melodies of violence

and hate

Her voice a stiff crackle as dark snakes coiling along my

neck whispering promises of what lies beyond the veil I

face

A dangling hour glass hangs threateningly as a

pendulum

Nursing me to such a ripe age to consume my flesh in

its coming day and indulge my blood as a tribute to her

ways decorating my bones in her buried home

A vain sheep nursed to slaughter to feed more to bring

death her never ending plate

She holds no keys to the eternal fires stolen by one who

overcame her hunger

A constant reminder sure to remind her of being

plundered

Creating a symphony of a vulgar hiss reminding her of

her own end

To forever starve in the great abyss

Left to her own device

LIFE'S TYPICAL DECOR

Pink curtains on a black frame, blood red glass cracked
splattered with purple paint. Gray walls fading white
half-finished halls decked with half crushed skulls.
Dark brown oily dirt floor blood-stained ceiling
sprinkled with love. Liquor slashed air calling of silent
specters staring. No words but the stretching eyes that
burned images on my wanting flesh. I dream of the land
I shall lie in. Mine grave is the path of the leopard's
prowl. Where is mine sword, mine shield, the armor
I dropped in that state of infernal fear? Where is my
light my hold among the fringes of tattered curtains
that now cower before the deathly cold? Who am I in
this place where the dead sing with shallow echoes of
hell?

A JOKE CALLED LOVE

Oh, what is this beautiful thing that comes in the beat

of a heart?

That is known far and wide and is put the world's

favorite treat

Tall tells that come across a barren land that holds so

dear to its myth

A darkened place of no retreat a bitter land of no

remorse to be

Acid that falls from a bleak dark sky

That eats at the strongest just so they may die

Upon this founded rock is the sulfur of the bitterest

lies

In which the beating of a heart is the cold chant of

our oldest lie

In which no one could say of its true face for its face is

a beast that eats the hearts of man

Ha funny this thing called love it is but a joke

If love be so strong that truth be but weak

The only one that is pure can hold such a dear thought

Yet this is the founding love, but in man, it is not

Oh, cry out you fools to this thing you trust

It stabs your side and brings you only to your old friend

lust

HELL, HATH NO FURY COMPARED TO THEE

To my old friend whom I trusted that taught me of
beauties bitter stab of vanity
To whom reveres as a crystal river that turns into rage
and casts those unwanted logs upon the oil streaked
beachside
I write this warning and poem to you
Mists of old do proclaim of this evil that continues
to eat true beauty as the acidic nature of time upon an
ancient mural
The power that brought love her strength is surely
drained in this vain woman's unholy glow
The rage of righteous love who screams injustice as
vanity runs her through
The death of love makes toil of a burdened heart
forever grows
Often, I wonder if she were a great actress that made
me a fool or were she a flower that turned bitter from
the fungus she grew as she waded in a cesspool
Nonetheless her character cannot be denied
Surely, she shall give birth to snakes that lie
Surely, she is revered by winter in her presence so that
winter can help stay cold
Whether the celestial beauty hide in shame of her

beauty or the reek of her vanity is the truth of her

flight

Though her skin be so smooth and true her speech

contains the hiss of a hungry snake that lures weary

men their doom

Surely a swan cannot match her grace, yet a swan's

heart is far from her for black as coal it beats once a day

Though her eyes gleam like emeralds the empty hole

behind them clouds men's minds with poisons that

forever renew

Her kiss greatly desired is the alcohol that brings

deaths desire

Her hair as smooth and long as willows branches yet

weary hearts it tangles

Legs so long and true to the spider's webs she will weave

on you

Hell, hath no fury compared to her stare

Surely hell hath a queen she has shown

Whilst Satan stole human innocence she completed the

task by robbing God's gift of beauty and gave birth to

vanity

Hell awaits her grand return to her thrown; the

world shall smile with beauties return that she stole

Yet in all her splendor life teaches this simple lesson;

Though the boost of her beauty is grand and all, of

this rare art that God gave her, is lost with age and

shall be such a bitter blow

I must profess my thanks for her gift to me

A knowledge and word of truth of her corrupted ways

I thank you for that sting of bitter report that taught

me your godless ways

Let this story of hellish report move the souls that

know not of the murder of this dead saint called love

let not these words grow weary and old

UNCERTAIN TIMES

I looked to the fog skewed window and found but a
reflection of my foggy vision of a dying world I would
rather abandon. I sought my reason for existence
and I could not find her. I am draining of my will
to remain in this hell like a waiting room where only
faded outdated sticky shopping catalogs are the means
of entertainment. Waiting to speak to some supervisor
to hand out my resignation and retire prematurely to
some unknown beyond those black curtains yet I stay my
hand once I heard that no rest is there for quitters
but endless torment for those who hate the game. We
are forced to play because of the rules of existence. We
are told to live our lives simply because it's our destiny.
We are told to enjoy our positions because the blessed
will see eternal pain one day and others below us our
crushed more. I can't understand how one takes delight
and sadistic joy in the agony of others so how is this
positive positioning a means to comfort our agony. Like
two crimson falls dictating years of my soul bleeding
from broken windows. I seek to spew my suffering in a
torrent of my life force staining the world with my
rebellion to this twisted state of existence. To find
comfort in the seductive shadows and let eternity
go by in the deepest slumber. To let go of these cruel

strings of destiny, dictating my every move. Painting

a plastic smile corroded by tears procured through

the pain of the stables that nailed it there. Forcing

happiness on the unwilling.

A FLOWERS LAYERS

Black rose set before me, the lush red tipped petal lips
parting sweet words trimmed with golden speech.
Tender slim figure blending in midnight. Moonlight
spots beauties goddess in flight. Melting in the black
velvet sheets of shadow, mine heart stalker. My most
fierce warrior. Run as swift soft wind yet quick to turn
vengeful and sunder. Dark seas hide a smooth figure,
mistress of the cold sea with volcanoes heart burning.
Dark eyes, the void consume ethereal plunder. Drinking
my soul, embrace my dreams sung of old. Be the night in
which my heart's light does glow.
I peel the layers from my mind, opened with a soft knife,
putrid thoughts as the onion gently wafting as the
cold salt water spewing on the wafting sand burning
with the fire-tipped suns fingers stroking it's sharp
leathered back piercing the sky with anguished lives,
don't want to hear, close your eyes, ears, nose, remove
the tongue, peel the skin and leave. Hand on my head
to peel back the eyes least the ugly truth leaves my sight,
my dreams are your eternal fright. My nightmares are
your unrecognized realities and the judgment to come
is the chaos I wish to taste upon the tongue yet this
vampire's thirst will leave me to hold your torch and
reveal my own treachery that I must seek absolution in
my flesh's leave.

BLACK BANKS

I nary noticed the cold bitter bite of a winter wind
that held me in her cruel sway but sought to embrace
her numb deathly hold in the blackest winter. I sought
to find peace in her embracing pain. The warmth of
life lingering in the blood splattered snow a vain hope
caught in the countenance of the night's deathly grim
visage. I sought to hold tight to the hated chill and
cool the burning hate that bubbled in the depths of
my embittered soul. I saw her clinging to the foggy
night seeking to corrupt me to know her betrayal all
to know the fate that I embrace. I seek to know not the
memories that I cling to as the frozen tears that refuse
to break free from the broken soul. I refuse to bleed but
hold in the fate handed by the rage that was born in
my creation, that never knew rest till the grave does
claim my wayward soul. I know no rest but as a banshee
glide across the banks of the black river that could not
hold. I sought to be devoured in the abyss but found
only myself caught staring myself in the blackened eyes
that felt no remorse but sought to leave behind the
last traces of my humanity in its murky depths. To find
solace in burying the torment that has brought me to
my scarred knees and left me knee-deep in the dead. I
only pray for release that I might know love no more
and be left in my sorrow.

BLOOD OATH BY THE DROWNING POOLS OF LOST FAITH

I sought you to shores of lost souls that did wash up
bloated with bitter hate that did afloat to these black
shores. I saw your soul's death upon a blackened cross of
false promises that sought to escape the founding love of
Christ to the lies of false prophets that made our lord's
suffering but a blurry vision and our founding lukewarm
pools of our former selves. I saw you die slowly, nothing
to do but witness soul's demise to return to the black pits
of former life only but a sad shell of the glorious saint I
once grew to love and nary receive the kindled embrace.
I hateful desire for the being I once so badly desired. I
learned the double-edged sword of love to cut deep into
me and learned to hate these yearnings that embittered
me. I sought to drown the desires to honor your hate
of my creation. The cruel punishments I sought out to
bear on myself, swearing on blood to deny the very cry
of my soul so deep down. I sought to punish myself with
the razor, I swore upon the pink tears my body and soul
did seep into the drain that I did flow. In my madness, I
drank deeply of my life fluids to swear an oath that love
shall never embitter my heart with her poisonous wrath.
A bittersweet treat, my life fluids I learned the delectable
flavor of life. Not to embrace it but devour its sweet

salty nectar and know its splendorous delight on the palate. I knew only hatred from this day so I sought to freeze that humanity to escape the voided madness of my embittered soul.

ETERNAL REPRISE

Beware the land where our ways are laid bare, our truths to haunt our self-wrought curse, the dark roads erupted in mists of denial the guilty flock in fleshy piles. Stocked by our grim visages that turned us to bathe in endless hatred. We bear the mark of Cain to remind us of this prison we did create. We shall all be accountable, rather as the monster that lurked in the night, her victims wrapped up so tight. Or lost innocence that sought to roam the fog-choked streets in endless hate. No forgiveness to quench the flames, no escape from the empty shell that lurks the dark corners but forever on the pain she'll embrace and seek death in the shed blood of the sick shades, that come to hear their accusations and accept their punishment for the eternal reprise. Fear not fool? Until you bear witness in the blood gilded glass you used to sheer, you will not know your end till you understand that humanity has no innocence, no peace, no release from its self-inflicted curse. We either burn with sadistic glee or for an unending thirst for blood stained revenge. We are the monsters, ever seeking a victim or burning revenge in our eternal reprise.

INNOCENTS PIT

There comes from a place deep within the chasms of humanity's darkest hell-born not from the rebellious fallen angel but the hatred born deep within all us born from the time of the Nephilim who ruled with the cold bitter hatred that betrayed innocence at the earliest levels. Where death did seek our race out but for the survival of one man who betrayed the hate so entwined in our souls. We sought to squander our petty evil but it is born in every child and this demon does betray the irony lost upon innocence that never sought light but died so early. His birth in the deepest of our woes does betray us to self-destruction and his eyeless gaze sneers in delight of his self-destructive nature. Know you this demon that sings in the pitch blackest of nights. The death of love before it is kindled in the fiery revelation of life's delights. Do you know the child of darkness that bears so deep in the tar cesspools of human ancestors? A seed so deep to dig it out would slay all but the basest human emotions and deliver us to a void that no escape can bear light in its anxious arms that hold us tight to our immortal deaths. He comes for you, no you not your doom on the waning wind with the stench of fate's cruel hands that hold us to our hellish dreams. Darkness has a name and he is called aborted innocence a mere child clothed in the rags of

human insecurities.

A WOMAN'S THIRST

I bled that she might drink deeply of the poison that
runs in my veins that she might taste the pain left to
rot in me,
I held my head high with a subtle smile of the waste
that my soul sank in,
the cesspool of my existence a mural and testament to
bring the hated feelings left deep in me.
A six-inch incision in the heart where the spout spewed
the life-giving love I sought to devote in the foolish
endeavor to feel human.
I sought to know the cage where I left my humanity,
that I might forget the hell my life was sprung from.
I looked for deliverance but found only hateful respite
and false accusations delivered with grins,
I dreamed that I slaughtered these deathly visages that
held me in awe of hate.
I sought to remove these demons from my mind but
could never free myself from their chains,
To be free of genetic disposition to position my neck in
open view of her razor to allow the slow draining, the
milking of my essence to punish me for what I was born.
She knew my desire to be her servant, she knew my
disposition that nature placed me to make me in the
position to be slain only to remove the heart to add to

her collection of victims.

The steady rhythm of their beating music to her wicked

ears to give purpose to sow destruction among mankind

as petty revenge to assuage the ache of her own heart.

Long ago her soul withered as a plant not

irrigated, seeking love so now when it comes, she only

devours and leaves the husk.

Nothing more than a black widow with and endless

thirst.

LOVES CASKET FEAST

Her cries kindled on the proverbial uncertainties of
enkindled love suffocated with a drought of rage. A
candle lit with faithless devotion unbridled in the
warmth of a yearning soul that knew not kinship but
a roaring hatred disguised in loving jostling amidst
the hissing of the serpent's call. Only amidst the
blackest pitch of darkness can unyielding love know its
light devoured in the coldest void. I know not where
the tunnel does end with light but feel the soft soil
lovingly cascade on an empty casket that holds the
remains of where my heart once did claim existence; but
is naught but ash to sprinkle on in a taunt ceremony
by the happy couples that take glee in the suffering
that false love is naught to know. The raven does cry
to feast on the gore they left to the specters to hold
laughter at this shell of a soul. Yet the bitter innards
do spew upon the ashen ground, it is a feast among
vultures who take to know the taste of its vain soul.
Vultures knew love in its kind hatred that mocked its
devotion and loyalty and blasphemed honor in its wake
yea its very core. Feast birds of the blackened air, feast
upon the innards that decorate your unholy city of
vain, love left without penance but became a sight of
endless death a body left a casket of its own demise yet

this masquerade of celebrated lust shall come to the

disease in which they feasted on the remains of love

unbridled and they shall become the dinner of blight

and disease.

MY WORLDS MERGER

Laying on a couch, the world's droll strolling by. The world is spinning, the rooms upside down, not sure where I am but seeking conformity in this misconstrued landscape peeling from the back of heavy lids. The floor is melting the wall shaving. I can't tell the difference from sinking or floating but what's it matter, I am in heaven while the demon's laughter takes me and I just don't care for all the world has passed away. The clock is ticking, at least I think or is it mocking my time slipping. I got lost in this place, I want to go back but never stay. I want to dream without this killing aid but I cannot free myself from all the dreary of decaying desert. I wonder but I am not lost when I have no place to locate. I can lay my head nowhere in reality but drift from lot to lot without leaving my home. I sought to rest in transcending but the devil follows with his hellish choir. Tell me the smoke drifting by was not lost history, that this paradise does not mock with a false pretense of escape. I sought vacation but found I could never leave this fantasy world where all is safe but no real comfort sinks her teeth in the throat to drain life from the empty veins drained by lovely reality. I cry in rivers and bathe in gritty sands that bear their sting in coming home to the life I sought to escape. The blood that shed, cannot pay for release, no price in deaths veins that so long ago drained me. I am kept a prisoner in one world or the other never meant to collide and yet reality and escape merge to one. No longer a place to go but lie in the torment of cruel mergers of insanity that orders submission. No hiding from escape, no deliverance from the shadow of light in twilight's bane. I seek true escape, I seek the end to existence yet immortal in life or death my plea falls on deaf ears that seek to escape my echoed cries. My existence is only mute.

NO MERCY, NO ESCAPE

A black pearl in a cupped hand to pool the shadowed
thoughts in a blended hurricane seeking refuge from
a choir of hate-filled voices that haunt the echoed
footsteps of my dire plots to deliver myself of blood
infused poisoned life seeking a torment that ends in a
shadowed call from the darkest chasms of unforgiving
rage the child that haunts me day and night. I am held
captive by violated innocence that will never give rest
till the death of the violator is cast upon a lead cross
gilded with his own bowels. Stripped as decorative ropes
tying his filth upon my revenge, no nails but the bones
across the heart where darkness forever spews. I cast m
y eyes to this Child's hateful rue, desiring only rest yet
he haunts me to no end, where the guilty pay with their
lives in poetic ironies to know their punishment is but
justices' cruel hand deep in their souls prying loose the
verdict of their demise from the cesspool that is their
bodies that linger in a black shadowed corner where
their darkness shall be their chains and the very evil
that hid their crimes will chain them unmercifully to
a mural of their victim's blood, guts, and bones to feel
the results of their unforgiving ways. My screams give
him life yet I cannot yield the silent accusations that
bring this demon to life. I cannot free myself from my

own tortured thoughts. My avenger has become my imprisonment. My "redeemer" has caught me in a web of my own hate. I cry out a release to the one who promises vengeance yet his cold hackled laughter holds me deep. His knife cuts deep, his eyeless gaze bears no soul and his manifestations are a product of my endless pain. I cannot escape from his grip, he holds me to my blood oath that gripped my soul. My words often betray a hunger for love that is vacant in the gaping hole where a heart did once beat till sacrificed on a black altar where ravenous dogs did take delight in its demise. Am I human? I cannot tell anymore. I am lost in this dirt less grave where no walls, nor chains adore but trapped I am.

THE LYING MIRROR OF TWO WORLDS

This fix I get from the cruelest addiction, I sought
to know your every once, a blood boil that scolded my
dreary bones in the ache of your presence. The grace
that I sought to know in your loving presence brought
about a hated drug addiction. Your every move and
thought is a crown upon my love's embrace. The unholy
attraction to your every action, a woman that holds
no competition is the life I bore to desire to mend with
your fire paved soul. This overdose that kills my every
waking moment left me a shell, I cannot steal away
from your ghost. I feel not the slightest tinge of your
presence but you are burned deep into my mind and left
a decayed love that never frees me from its cruel grasp.
Like a skeletal existence I once did know, I desire to
peel away yet I left behind what made me whole. This
bloodlust to seek your life to know inside is the poison
that left me soulless in this eternal love-hate. I hate
you with the deepest rage upset by the empty place where
my innards rotted from never knowing your touch. You
burned me with the unfulfilled desire. You struck me
without a hand to leave a mark that none could bear
its sight but still, it bore into me a tick that left not
a drop of my essence but hollowed out without a drop

left to grace this shell. I am sick from the withdrawal of your presence and my honor bound me to bear away and though without honor and lust-stricken fools you sought to allow their filth to bind but the cesspool of their taint did leave you deathly. Though you felt their filthy touch and found the error of their ways I am left all the deader inside despite clinging to honor and respecting your revulsion of my presence. Let us be revolted of our ways and separate in my illusion of desire and no love shall I touch, filthy embrace I shall refuse till death take me to his lovely grave and your lust shall consume you till you are a widowed mess of bitter hate. Our connection only in our misery of opposite ends. The only connection I shall be given in the kind grave.

ESSAYS AND NARRATIVE POETRY

This portion of my works are still poetic in nature but more like an essay. I don't have a lot of them but the few I have are good reads and long. Some are narrative style poetry. Not much to say on these other than an expression made on how I feel. I have a unique perspective on looking at the world and I think these works really show it.

EMILY

The air was cold and seemed to freeze as if this day was merely a picture in time. A sense of electric anticipation tingled through Justin's nerves as he waited for the doorbell that would announce his childhood friend's approach. Memories long past invading his present concentration to days where discreetly leaving gum in unknown places was a fun game and her cries of redemption from its tangling power produced a roaring laughter. Barely a year younger she was as close as a sister and trust worthy as a brother. The engraved images of lost youth played at him wishing to take part back in these innocent days were broken only by a sudden light knock.

He was awakened from his dreaming and racing toward the door he opened it wide only to see with disappointment his mother with a handful of groceries. "Please help me dear" Quickly gathering the heavy burden and placing the food in the appropriate place his mother's smile haunted him as a sense of pride overcame her at her son's accomplishment of completing high school. A light kiss on the check left burning marks on his face and a groan of embarrassment as if a grinning audience stared in amusement "I am sorry honey, but I am so proud of you" A secret being of pride welled up in him he well hid as he complained of her rampant and repetitious remarks of his honors graduation. He then wondered why of all days that had been often repeated his only wish on his mind was for his close friend to give him escape from the ever-pressing walls around him.

There came a persistent and eager knock on the door that suggested that its answer be swift. Justin whipped the door open and there stood Emily's smiling face much more mature than the youthful blank expression she had as a child. Dancing about arms flailing as a chimpanzee in a green dress celebrating the capture of a golden banana she spat out some juicy gossip of young scandals she had to pronounce to the world of as dire news. Once again finding himself nodding at every word pretending to hear her he counted the "Oh my gods" to be at 32. "A new record" he barked in laughter. With her confused look he quickly changed the subject lest he endure a cold hard stare the rest of the night with an even more so juicy story that would hold the press.

After a few minutes of exchanged laughter over Mark Flute›s showering rain of stomach on the unsuspecting crowd below at the fall festival they headed out for Justin›s new car. Well, it was new to him anyhow. Justin growing up with not much had learned the value of appreciating what he did have and the hard work of summers he poured into his 86 Chevrolet. To him it was as grand as any car. The drive seemed so quick as they chattered over how the new Metallica had sold out and sucked compared to what

the used to be and other various intriguing aspects to life
that were to be forgotten the moment they were spoken.
Soon they pulled up to the old familiar pizza joint Pizza
Papa they patronized since childhood. This was their official
meeting place for celebrating whatever event might be going
on which usually was something every week. There were
many fine Italian foods they could order as well and since
tonight, was so special they were going to order the best
Pizza Papa could offer.

Joe Conti eagerly approached his two favorite customers
with a wink and a smile, he proclaimed "Well if it isn't my two
favorite love birds" Justin flaming at the checks objected
to this proclamation but almost with a light regret hidden
in his voice. A quick glance at Emily he noticed an almost
undetectable decrease in her smile at this and he began to
wonder inside himself. What caused that slight change in
her expression? Was she embarrassed as he was or did she
regret that the statement was not true? Why was it that he
kept turning red and so anxious around her now? He had
never had this trouble with girls before. He had always had
this magic touch and could master almost any girl he dated.

His confidence never failed him but for some reason her
presence made him anxious. Perchance it was merely that he
was leaving California for schooling in New York the very
next day. Yes, that must be it. It was simply the idea of leaving
her. As he pondered this, he was interrupted with Joe tapping

him on the shoulder. "What!" Justin jumped, "Well young Justin hear was lost in his thoughts dreaming of the wild parties, exam cramming nights, chasing girls and college life that he left us already. Wake up Justin" Joe laughed. "What would you like to drink Justin" Emily's polite grin took him in for a second and he responded "Oh, Pepsi will be fine" "I will have a coke" Emily replied.

Joe swiftly left and Justin let out a sigh. «Well, this is the last night of our little spot for a good while. Yeah I suppose it is» Emily glumly replied. It just seems like it was yesterday we barely met back in Ms. Bean›s class. Justin said «Yeah you poured glue down my dress and swore Casper the ghost did it. She replied in a monotone voice. After a moment of silence, laughter burst out of them both without control. After they regained their composure several more stories of their most savored childhood memories were exchanged and a fondness that grew started to amend them.

He took a moment to gaze into her jade green eyes that glared at him. They seemed to capture him in some sort of emerald prison. Her small pale round face reminded him of a full moon lighting the night sky as the dim lights bounced off of her. Her slender long fingers tapping nervously on the checkered table entranced him. Her small mouth tightly shut made him dare to provoke her speak to hear that soft buttery voice.

"Now what are you going to be dining on tonight" Joe

replied as Justin jumped. "Wake up Justin. What would you like to eat?" Joe replied. So entranced he was by things he had never noticed about Emily before he was startled. "Umm I would like to try the chicken croquettes with roasted pepper sauce" replied Emily. "I will have the Italian Style Meatloaf" Justin replied "Excellent choice I will have it right up" Joe replied eagerly. "So how are things going with Trevor Emily?" Justin asked. Emily shifted in her chair a little and her head dropped as she tried to hide a silent tear drop from the corner of her eye. "What's wrong?" Justin persisted "I caught him cheating on me with Jessica Thornton" She replied in a small hoarse voice. Anger and a strange sense of joy welled up in Justin as he moved in to hold her in his arms. "I am so sorry to hear that Emily" He held her small sobbing body in his arms and never had he felt such a warmth in his grasp. He ran his fingers through her long cheese nut brown hair and slowly rubbed her back in consolation for his close friend. After a few soothing words she regained her composure and sat back in her seat. "I am sorry for acting like such a baby. I need to grow up and get passed this." Emily said. "Don't worry about it. If you ever need a shoulder to cry on I will be here. You would do the same for me I am sure Emily" "Thank you so much Justin.... You are a true friend" Emily said in tearful voice" A dumb found stillness gripped the room like a tightly woven fist that strangled the restaurant. An echo almost seemed to hint at the dull walls. "So, what are you going to Major in anyhow?" Emily asked in a sly tone. "Well, I am not quite sure. I plan on getting my basic's out of the way and after that I may major in English. I have always wanted to be an author so I figured that would be a good avenue to pursue" Justin replied in a relief to break the silence. "You always had such a way with words Justin. You always seem to notice a lot of details in your surroundings. I think that would be a great career for you to pursue. What topic do you plan on writing?" "Well, I was thinking that I would delve into fantasy. I have always loved the subject. It gives me a break from reality and lets me extend my world and train of thought." "I see" Emily responded.

Their food arrived so they began too silently and slowly eat their food. Almost as if regretting having to finish it as it might mark the end of their long uninterrupted friendship once Justin left. She seemed to glow as he glanced to her from time to time and a swelling agony of loneliness pained his heart at the thought of having to leave such gentle creature. He fought to keep his composure but it simply tore him up to hold it. The question that had haunted him floated in the air once again Have I fallen in love with Emily? He thought to himself. He looked at her with an intensity that seemed to pierce her very soul that she almost caught him staring. His heart beat faster by the minute, his breath seemed shorter, and the idea of losing her became as unbearable as death itself. "Yes" he humbling admitted under his breath. He had fallen for the very girl he once called sister. It only made since that he would have fallen for her. Look how perfect she was. She seemed to be flawless and without mar in every aspect. He felt he could capture the moon and give it to her as a symbol of his undying love. Nonetheless he would be leaving tomorrow. What could he do? Emily and he often spoke of how long-distance relationships never work. How could he possibly care for her if he was all the way in New York? It was too late to change his plans and he had dreamed of going to college in New York. This internal pressure was bearing to great of a weight for him to stand and he was about ready to scream.

"Wake up Justin" Emily said in a cool voice. "You keep straying off tonight what is going on in that head of yours." Nothing much just anxious about college" Justin replied in a still voice. "I was thinking Emily that we should stay for desert since this is our last night together" Justin's almost trembling voice broke out. "Yes, I think that would be a great idea" "Joe" Justin called out. "Will you bring us two chocolate mousses" "Sure thing Justin... It's on the house considering it will be a while before I see you again" "Thank you very much Joe." To get something free from Joe was quite an accomplishment as Justin had once seen him quiver over giving a dollar to his own daughter. Joe may have been a bit cheap but he was a good man and always a good mentor to Justin and Emily. A few moments later the grand sight of two delicious chocolate mousses appeared from behind the double doors. "Here you are. Enjoy!" Justin finally could not stand it any longer he took Emily by the arm crossed over to her and leaned up next to her small lips and imparted a gentle kiss that soon turned into a compassionate lingering hold. She held him tight as they enveloped one another in a passionate embrace that flew up the grand sparks of what lay dormant for so long. She then tenderly asked in his wanting ear.

«Justin, when are you going to wake up? Huh Justin replied. «I said when are you going to wake up? You are

day dreaming again. Oh! Sorry. It was all another day dream. It's as if he were stuck in a desert forever chasing mirages. As they both slowly finished off the deserts Emily spoke almost as if reluctant. Justin, can I ask you a question? What Oh never mind. As they both got up to leave Justin left a generous tip and told Joe goodbye. The drive seemed like an eternity yet so short. As she said her final goodbyes and started to fade disappearing in the darkness he called out to her. Wait, Emily! I have to tell you something before I leave." "What is it, Justin?" she replied with a sly yet reluctant smile" "Emily, I love you!" Justin yelled as a deafening echo ringed in his ears. The very air quivered as a response to what he declared. Emily only starred with a long sad smile that pierced him like a million knives. "Justin, when will you wake up? Please just wake up. You are dreaming again. Just let me go in peace."

by her response everything seemed to melt around him. An engulfing darkness that consumed everything around him enclosed about until only she remained as a fading ghost into the recesses of his mind. He fell for a while in this darkness until finally after a long scream he awoke from the nightmare sweating excessively. He found the same empty bed that he had been sleeping in for years. The memories came back like a tidal flood. Emily was dead. Tonight, was the twentieth anniversary of her death. The very night he left for New York a drunk driver killed her and a friend that were headed for the very restaurant they had their last meeting in. He was told what her last words were. "Justin.... Wake up, please Justin, wake up" No one knew why she said this. It was just assumed some last-minute jumbled words at the shock of death. It only seemed to him as if death gave a cruel revelation of his becoming to her as a final mocking blow to her. The drunk driver was Trevor himself. He lived and he only served for ten years. No punishment would be too great for that murder Justin thought to himself. He stumbled through the jumbled mess of trash on the floor knocking over a vodka bottle.

He noticed thirty messages on his answering machine. He

mashed the button and deleted most of them without even listening until he heard his mother's voice poured out. "Justin this is your mother I am just calling to check up on you. I haven't heard anything from you in months and no one knows where you have gone off to." I know Emily's death was hard on you but son it's been twenty years now. I just wish you could wake up from this and live your life. This isolation can't be good for you.... I just wish you could let her go and rest in peace." The answering machine clicked off as he heard a low sigh. The trimming of a sob could be heard in her voice. He had not cried since Emily's death. Not even at the funeral. It's as if he forgot how to cry least the memory of her seep out of him. He picked up an old faded photo of her and just starred with unwavering lips hearing her words echo in his mind from his dream. The truth being he never really did tell Emily he loved her that night. He just could not muster up the courage and he had a feeling of the need to punish himself for it. He ran his course hand over his rough wild growing beard. He debated rather or not to shower. It had been over a week but he simply did not care. He silently got dressed in dirty old jeans, stained white shirt, and old shoes. It was said in scripture that the dead should bury the dead but as far as Justin looked, smelt, and felt he met those qualifications.

He took the long walk to the cemetery that he did yearly to visit her. The night lingered as a cold testament to the reality he faced every year and light wisps of fog crawled over the ground as venomous snakes. He stared

at the grave still unable to relieve the very pain of tears

that tried to fight their way through his hardened

defense. Slowly he bent to leave his token of love to her. He

laid a single lily on her grave. Lilly's were always her favorite

flower. As he laid it at her grave a small piece of paper that

was neatly put against her gravestone grabbed his attention.

It was a poem by Rosalyn R. Smith entitled Wake Up. He

slowly read the poem and as he did so a solemn tear filled

the corner of his eye and slowly dropped to the ground. He

finally, could be relieved of his punishment. He now knew as

if by miracle or coincidence that her death did not separate

him from his Emily. She would always remain inside him.

The contributions she made in him would never fade. It is

amazing how a simple poem could produce a single tear that

healed twenty years of constant pain. He walked home that

day no longer feeling the regret of an empty bed but of many

years to catch up on. A book to finish he had never started.

EMILY PART 2

A slow drooling day passes by as Justin leans in bent over like a dead willow tree begging of sweet rain to run her course down its dry boughs. Justin's valiant attempt to retain every bit of imagined decency pounding against a rock-hard resilience of pride. His garments implying his continued state of mourning he dares not leave for idle pleasure. His very presence seems to put a dull presence within the folds of his determined state of melancholy. An elderly gentleman takes notice of this most perfect picture of human hopes cruelest defeat and approaches with what almost seem a glide.

Beautiful day isn't it son. Justin looks up with the heinous dark circles about his sleep deprived eyes and with a scowl stares at the relentless old man. He is not in the mood for idle optimistic fools that encroach upon his misery. Justin knew that the optimistic secretly enjoyed human misery as some kind of sick pleasure at seeing someone more misfortunate than themselves. He was sure of this and was determined to resist the old man's attempts at conversation. The old man seeing his resistance is determined to get a word in. So, tell me young man what brings a youth such as yourself brought to the utter low state you present yourself in. Young man, Justin thought. Was this man blind or something? What's it to you. Justin replies coldly. Well

I have nothing better than to do than stroll the park
and pick on poor heartbroken young men with my overly
optimistic views on life. Justin looks up with one eyebrow
bent up. It seemed odd that his comment was a rebuttal of his
presumption on the old man's purpose. Just a coincidence and
nothing more Justin thought to himself. Justin decided he
had nothing better to do than entertain the elderly man
with his bitter views of life. Tell me old man. What is life
but emancipation from the simple pleasure of not having to
this redundant existence? How is it we go about surviving
simply for continued disappointments in life? We strive to
survive for what reason other than the sick pleasure of
watching others squirm to get past their unjust obstacles
to help us cope with our own dislodged hopes. What is the
point beyond this blank void in which we both love and
hate? To know these simple questions, one must truly come
to terms with what Hamlet truly meant when he proclaimed
"To be, or not to be, that is the question". All so repeatedly
quoted by many and no one seems to truly understand
the implications of what Hamlet was saying. It is all but
a pretty quote to the unobserved masses. Nothing beyond
the skin-deep ideas of what true meaning really is. The old
man seems unloved by these words and only lets out a quiet
chuckle. Does this seem all so amusing to you? You come
as you care but your amusement at my cost only proves the
misunderstood truth behind the optimistic heart. Am I dark

in my mourning of injustice or is the darker heart of the
optimistic the true villain. I do say that men of evil intent
do not come in black but the lightest garments. Satan hides
in light does he not? The old man sits with a gentle smile
on his face and speaks. Well, you do misinterpret greater
than you seem to realize young man. You view abstract
concepts without an ability to distinguish other truths
found in life. You say I enjoy your heart ache but I laugh
at simple ignorance of a misinformed soul. A laugh is not a
sick amusement for selfish absorbed people it is a challenge to
the dark forces of life that strive to take away our ability
to enjoy life to its fullest. It is a gift to give power to us to
overcome and simply this. True some individuals have sadly
capitalized on this for selfish purpose but that does not
make the tool any eviler than a gun fired by a criminal.
It is the human behind it that determines its purpose and
nothing more. True enough that Satan hides behind the
light but does that make the light any less good simply
because a force chose to misuse its purpose. The light is not
a tool of evil but is just as liable for misuse as any other
instrument of great power.

Justin then begins to find the conversation interesting
at these conjectures. He is still greatly reluctant to open
up but finds it to be a sure way to pass the time. The old
man, then brings up the question. Once again what troubles
your heart to cast a shadow as dark as yours. You have

spoken of your philosophy of life yet just as a light needs a source so does a shadow. Justin pauses for a minute only staring into the void in which his heart has plummeted. He thinks back to the day his heart died along with his love. He does not wish to confess that he was foolish enough to trust in something such as love so he cannot but remain as silent as the sullen lonely gravestone he visits every year. The old man sensing his reluctance to confess speaks. Well son from the depth of your state I cannot but say that it is lost love that drives you to the grave. What greater rot than love that is lost can be produced. The most powerful tool of good can often turn the sourest. Justin is surprised by this observation. Well yes... Justin quickly realizes his defenses softening and quickly reassures himself. It is not lost love so much but the idea that I had fallen into such a waste. What is love but a noble excuse to impose one's will on another human being. I believe in love as much as any other myth. Love is beautiful in its imagined purpose but no truer than the dead myths of the pasts. They are simple stories there to only entertain a dying world. Why believe in such a ridiculous thing as love? Men hunt women down like prey to simply devour them in their undying sexual compulsion. Women leaving a detailed scent, putting out traps and willingly becoming this prey simply to wrap a foolish man's heart in the chains of her imposing beauty and take everything he has. Men and women both think they have complete control but are only simple-minded fools entertaining their captivating delusions. They are but prey and hunter at the same time while they deceive themselves to think they are the hunter. Is there any difference to give chase to prey or to lay out traps for prey? It is all the same. Though one chases and the other lays out traps they are still both hunters and therefore are prey to each other. What is love but a bad joke of human delusion. The old man almost seems humored by the response. Well, I see your point but not always is the hunt for mere indulgence. Though the man does become prey to a woman's devices does he not enjoy the very thing that catches him? Though the woman is given chase does she not enjoy the affection that drives the man? You seem to see love in the light as being some selfish purpose that humans have need to fulfill but it is the pleasure of being caught and victim to the devices of another that fuels love. Is it selfish to desire to become possessed of another to please them? The pleasure in love is the joy of giving to the other, not receiving. While the man does get pleasure from making love to his wife he gets just as much pleasure if not more in providing for her. Just as much as the woman benefits from being provided for, she gets pleasure out of providing love for the man. The man gets the satisfaction of being wanted by her need for him as the woman finds satisfaction from him desiring her. This is the tie of love that holds people together no matter who they love. Gender does not matter and the same can be said of anyone for desire comes in all shapes and forms even if of the same gender. For true love this is truth anyhow. But it all goes back to the same idea of the wielder. Is love any less good if wielded by evil for the wrong purpose? It is almost as if some great art in marriage. You could say the saying "tie the knot" is more literal than people realize. The old man let's out hearty laugh. Justin almost feels what seems to be warmth coming from the old man.

Well, that may be true to the whole hearted but to those whose heart knows no function and it is simple myth to us. My heart cannot function. Take the old abandoned house for example. My heart is just as the old broken windows of an abandoned home. The house is no longer loved for its work of protecting its unappreciated occupants from the cruel threshold of nature. Left like some soulless haunt, left as a mere tomb stone to only be torn down by times merciless weight. The homes functions no longer able to hold life within its hollow walls. Only to receive the mocking blows of idle stones thrown by careless devils enthralled with the chance to wreak havoc on a decadent building no one cares for. What point but to tear it down and lament in its shattered remains. The old man does not stir but lays his kind eyes on Justin. The old man than responds to Justin's discussion. Well while the home may appear destitute and lonely is it not shown love by the markings of time upon its wall's? The careful lines marking the descendant's slow growth. The marks of love left from living within its halls. Is not the tombstone just as beautiful in its dedicated words? of the lost love as it is grieving? The damage done upon the building is not necessarily done in hate but shows the love of use. To be well lived in is how the saying goes. You speak that it has lost its purpose but cannot a house be repaired?

Can it not find love again and be restored? Should it be torn down? The foundation in which it was established can establish a new home. It is not so much the home itself that bears importance but the foundation. The ground in which it stands. That is the one established importance that can never truly be completely destroyed. It is either good ground or bad and that is all. The home is the heart but without the foundation it is unstable and nothing.

"There is some truth in your saying but your speech is likened to a man who tries to describe light to a man who has been bound to a cave all his life", said Justin. Though it may sound pleasant will it be pleasant when the light first sets upon the man's eyes? It will burn as hot as hell. The old man responds. Well, that may be true but in time he will adjust and the value of its result pays for itself. Justin responds. Well, I cannot see this light therefore I cannot realize its truth. All is black to me now. The darkness is what I know and can therefore understand. The old man responds. Well then do you seek the darkness or feel that you belong to it. You say you see the heart, love and life in these ways because of darkness. You cannot perceive any other truth simply because you cannot see this goodness in life. Young man it is not that you cannot see light but you have come to view it in its full intensity. You are blinded from looking into the sun so you look to the night in its darkness. You look at the home at night but in order to see the home you must have some source of light. Therefore, it must be by moonlight and starlight. Though you see it darkly and perceive clouds to obscure the sky you have been able to see a side to life with a certain light. You must not deny though that the moon is not the giver of light at this time but the light comes from the same source as the day. Because you looked at the sun in the eye it hurt you and you came to hate this light but do not realize that though you see the moon without recoil it is the same light that blinded you. This light is produced by nothing more than a big rock that reflects the ultimate source of light. This rock is dependable though and just as important. The ultimate source of life, light and order in the universe cannot be viewed with our human eyes without being hurt so he gave us a rock to reflect that light without hurting our eyes. This light provides hope in a dark world and guides us in our path. It is also, what makes the horrid night so beautiful. It is not the light or the dark alone that is beautiful but how the moon brings light to a dark world. Hope is how the stars reach us from the furthest corners of the galaxy. It is how they pierce the greatest depths of darkness to reach us. Though the sky may darken from the storm clouds we still have the reassurance that the moon and stars have not left us and will continue to light our path once the storm clouds recede. To put it simple Justin, your problem is not a lack of light it is your denial of the moon and stars existence despite the fact you see the world with their light and don't even realize it. You sleep in day light therefore you deny the day time exists and therefore you cannot perceive the light you see by at night is the very thing you deny. That is what is funny. You believe in the most absurd ideas and cannot realize it because you resolve to close your eyes and are too afraid to open them and see things for how they really are. Justin is shocked by what the man has just told him. He cannot respond and stares off into space for a long while. Suddenly he realizes that he had never given the old man his name. Hey how did you know my name anyhow? The old man does not respond. Justin turns to ask again only to realize the man is gone. A shiver runs down Justin's spine but figures he must have grown board with the conversation and just left while he was thinking. I... I must have mentioned my name and just forgot...that's all. He then resolves to go back to his mourning but cannot get the words out of his mind.

NIGHTMARE AND MUSINGS OF A BROKEN HEART

I must confide in my writing at this time to preserve
what many would call a curse or displeasing event
meant to be passed as waste. Upon falling asleep to
the writings and philosophical views of The Book of
the Courtier it came to my attention in a dream...
not so much a dream but a nightmare with the most
unusual of qualities that would inquire many to ask
what credentials it could boost to such an ambiguous
dream. Not long upon my slumber the unusual chance
of a dream caught onto me. Not so much a dream I
repeat but a nightmare of unusual properties. I found
myself looking inside as if mine eyes had turned from
the outward to the inward to peer into the darkest
crevice of my body. The container that holds the soul
prisoner until his final resting place is determined.
This creature called the heart in which many profane
their trust, yet have only later been betrayed despite
his kind demeanor and stance. No this is a creature
whom I locked away for such treachery to never again
see the light of day and embrace an artificial death
behind prison walls of bitterness. This jailor had
become jailed, yet from my human error of my making I
found myself unable to imprison my offender as he was

an unfortunate necessity in my function. With that
defined I continue to what I refer to my nightmare
in, which the only explanation I can determine
without defining why this is the case other than the
subconscious knowledge that I am not permitted full
access to, is that a crack within my heart's walls big
enough to show the decayed remains of what I forsook,
renounced, and damned the beating bastard. It was just
as much a part of me as an arm or leg and yet so much
more but lack of trust could not let me infringe upon
my contract forbidding contact with this creature of
habit. Alas as it is known to any man, he who fights
his true self will only lose in the end. This curse of
an obsession with cupid's sting, this helpless character
of a romantic haunts my very existence and leaves me
to wither without the alcoholic addiction of love's
touch. I saw within this chamber the very scars that
dug deep into the core of my very being corrupting my
soul. This past time and various symbols of my youth,
flashing before me sections and memories that had long
died only to be raised to bring bitter tears to my weary
eyes. This floating about observing the very images
before me filled me with terror for reasons I cannot
explain other than the sixth sense I have thus held
telling me the meaning. The power that cracked the
walls to my heart then inverted me pulling me, taunting

me, warning me or whatever its purpose was to show the drastic reality of what was before me. I could feel as if literally being inverted upside down shaken as a well-worn doll out of spite. At that moment what my memory tells me watching from above at some point my father upon a couch alone. My utter pain, grief and pitiful sorrow drowning me in a sea of regret wishing to speak to, to hold in comfort, to cry our most bitter feuds out in a pool of reconciliation but an invisible wall of the chaos and curse that has visited my family, bars us from this and leaves us punished for a crime in which I cannot reveal in my ignorance of its nature. The haunting presence of this world my soul was thrust in perhaps it was even the eyes of the soul within the imprisoned heart screaming at such great lengths to tremble the course inner prison walls of my heart and reach the secular area of logic within my heavy mind. The terror of this mangled creature I have long forgotten, except the various protests of whispers that manage through the bitter deep walls of my heart. This truth of insight in the message conveyed by what I can only determine as a message from God has shaken me to the core in which I realize much pain is the absence of my one true love. My maker who held me in my darkest sway during the tear-filled nights that led me to a deep slumber. My heart whom I encased was the receiver of his love letters. Although the heart is betrayed, it was the only means in which I could convey the love that the soul was so highly intoxicated by. As I have oft said in this letter to myself, he who fights himself will always lose. My success at isolating my betrayer has at the same time ensured my failure. Brought to my knees by a simple picture into my worm wrought heart. A woman that haunts me for the rest of my days. It is all but a leash by my true love to see the destruction of my very being. The helplessness in attempting to revive this seems to me at a loss. I stare off into space wondering how I might achieve such a victory but alas I may not call it such. To call mercy a victory is a fool's folly. Should I ever achieve freedom from the binds of this predicament I shall call it a mercy by a God who sees no fault but broken children. Children he goes to are not pretty faced or grand in any such way but savage beasts made by nature and environment. Beasts that he may tame to one day devour the world of his enemies. His glory is found in hopeless works. Is it so grand that a sculptor should make a statue that glazes the hardest eyes? Though such a work is blessed and appreciated the work that draws nations is the sculptor who makes such a work of art from a single toothpick out of the ugliest hardest stone. Upon such inspection of this rock as the master reveals the potential of its rock easel when the glittering shine of the hidden diamond sparkles with the new made sculpture. Such a beauty marble may be but a sculpture made from a single toothpick out of the ugliest hardest rock that ends with a pure diamond work of art is the very essence of God's work. It is the impossible that draws the attention of kings and queens. Should a regular work of beautiful art be created the art is more remembered often than the artist. Yet the diamond sculpture is not so breathtaking as the artist who conquered the most stubborn of elements with one of nature's weakest tools. In closure to this observation in one of the most peculiar natures of God I must confess the need to cry out on my broken-down knees the very tears I held back. The dam in my heart and soul breaks and bitterness can only hold so long.

UNNECESSARY DIVISIONS

Had a thought. It seems a lot of the negative stereotypes used against other groups are often the same allegations made by the racists of the other groups. All racists have the same mentality. So those of us who don't care about race should all agree that the negative stereotypes of all races tend to be the characteristics of racists. Racists I think are even self-hating to some degree because they are mentally broken. Racism is not natural in humans. It has to be conditioned in them. We don't see black horses and white horses battling each other so why the hell can't we at least be like animals who identify themselves as a species rather than a color of species.

This is why I hate sports. It's just one color versus another color. One state or city against another state or city. People are viciously supportive of their teams in which it comes to violence and what for? A fucking game? Seriously I have no faith in humanity in their severe emotional gravitation toward a "team". There is no opposing team in humanity and we should all look out for one another rather than using divisions to keep us from working together.

The difference in religion is also a dividing factor. There are divisions even within the divisions. This is also what is wrong with Capitalism as it creates division among people causing them to compete. Rather than improve themselves they tend to dissolve into cheating and sabotage. What good is the competition it, it causes us to work against our own species? Socialism encompasses compassion and cooperation as opposed to competition.

Even sexuality is a tactic to use against people. Some people feel more comfortable with same sex relations or feel they are another gender. Regardless of how we feel about this we have no right to judge any more than they would to judge us but typically it is the heterosexual community that has been feared into thinking different sexualities are dangerous when in reality these are just people trying to live their lives. They have a right to their life so long as they do not hurt anyone. It is the pedophiles, necrophilist and those engaging in bestiality that are crossing a line as the victim is not consenting or unable to consent as well as problems with disease. We can see logical reasons as a society to restrict these practices as the victim and health issues that affect society are affected as well as the perpetrator. The religious right painted a picture of hatred towards health sexualities to further division and control over their people.

Now there are some aspects of society and business

in which capitalism is good but it has to be well regulated and the business should know the purpose of its existence is to provide a product or service at a fair price. The quality must be high and the employees must be well paid to live a normal life without being slaves.

Most wars were created by the oligarchy to make themselves rich and they always use the people's divisions to make us fight each other instead of our rich overlords. The mega rich must one day become extinct if we are to ever evolve as a society.

We must stop being a self-fulfilling prophecy of this doomsday cult most religions have established. We expect the world to end so we carelessly go in that direction without making effort to preserve our world for the future. This is what I have come to see as true terror as I was once obsessed with the world ending. I kind of do want it to end because of how I see how fucked up it is but I think we should try to preserve the future and establish a fair and comfortable life for everyone.

First, we must accomplish this in our own nation and once we have created this system we must use peaceful methods to spread the good ideas that project society toward a healthier cleaner future. Bill Gates was right. Socialism is the only way we can preserve and save our planet from a self-fulfilling prophecy of destruction.

WISDOM BEGETS THE SIGHT OF FOLLY

It only occurred to me recently the changes that
so dramatically alter my life. It seems like yesterday
certainty was established in the world in which I knew
myself and the wiles of my world were confined to a
certain set of ideas that shaped the world. As I grow
older these certainties receded into a certain chaos
of my old foundation dissolving into a puddle of
ideologies that are no longer familiar to me. If I am
to be honest with myself I must say that I was gifted
with enough wisdom and knowledge to understand
just how ignorant I really am. I've always pondered the
meaning of my existence which to the extent I often
wonder rather I exist substantially or am a blundering
shell seeking validation in a world I have often felt
alien to. Love has always been a foreign emotion to me
that comes so rarely I often wonder of its possibility.
I have spent the greater part of my life pondering the
very reason I exist in a world obsessed with the trivial
and the bane of individuality. Where can I even to
begin to describe the state of my maddened mind that
has sought out its own destruction that I might
not bear the company of myself which I could never
stand. It often feels as life is but a fog that obscures

the certainty and absolution of my place in this world leaving me to question my own humanity. The insatiable desire to be perfect defies what it means to be human and I often find myself hiding in obscurities to avoid being placed in a state of chaotic imperfections. This endless roulette of seeking reason behind my many flaws has me constantly questioning my worth as a living being. It fills my mind with pronounced judgments of mankind in its ability to function healthily. With the terminal illness of man forever unsatisfied in his lusts for wealth, I am disgusted to no end at the hateful exchange of cruelty and ambition that people are never short of. The defining moment that has led me to this conclusion of misery is the constant restless rage that burns within me with flames that never quite consume. This state of agony has brought to my attention the need to find like-minded intellectuals that I might perhaps find some sort of belonging in humanity that I might not be alone. My severe distrust of women or more so humanity itself has left me indifferent to the opposite sex but not without great desire. I have often found myself obsessing over women like a mere school boy with a permanent crush on just the possibility of finding a likeminded woman. My fantasies of finding such a mate leaves me with much to desire to no avail as I lack an understanding of what exactly it is that

I look for in a companion. This inconsistency of desire versus fear of rejection or bitter incompatibility leaves me often in great turmoil. I must say I am at a loss as to what I really want so I often find myself in a perpetual stalemate. There was a time a woman whom I revered as a sweet mother like figure that prophesied that I was special and God had someone special for me. I both loathed this and revered it with anticipation as my mother left a bad taste in my mouth for her indifference while growing up but alas I often idolized the idea of finding such a woman feeling that I am missing a key component in my very creation. I often fear my status will leave me an undesirable and once again rejection lurks its ugly head to mock me. When I was young and filled with idolized imagination of what I believed to be true love I found only bitter humiliation as the two objects of my desire found me highly objectionable. These girls were sure to mock me of all the inadequacies my perfectionist mind bore into me convincing me that no woman could love such a freak as they deemed me. The one "true" love I sought out preferred an older man only to separate shortly thereafter and seek the lust of the other girl whom my attention turned to after I found no acceptance in her. These elements created a kind of alchemy in me that devastated me to the point of severe isolation and hatred of the very emotions that betrayed me. In order to protect myself from these unknowns and uncertainties I adopted a severe brutality of continued abuse to prevent these emotions from coming to fruition. I went so far as to continue severe emotional self-abuse laced with physical abuse from time to time. In order to prevent a rehash of past events I ended up causing more harm than alleviation.

Having high functioning autism has turned every form of relationship into a cruel guessing game I never wished to endure but does not change the fact that deep down inside I still desire a woman to compliment me into a better person. My infatuation with women has turned them into sort of an enigma that I wish solved. They have this sort of mystery and power about them that leaves me wanting to simply be around them. Alas I digress into what I see as a shallow desire but again the negative stigma of my past leaves me more in confusion as to what I really want. It often amazes me though that the greatest mystery of our lives is our own body and soul. It is so much easier to judge another's character when a person must forever be at a loss for the reasoning behind our own thoughts and actions. We often seem to drift into autopilot and in our slumber of consistent lifestyles we no longer realize why it is we make the choices we make yet always on the guard of the actions and words of others without questioning our own motivations. Are we products of environment, genetics or the whim of chaos that is our ever-changing minds. We grow to love the status quo all the while hating it with the utmost contempt. We often want the world to change without wanting to change ourselves as change always hurt. At that thought I have to ask myself if I really want to continue this facade of complacency or seek to evolve beyond sugar coating everything in life or hiding from the world. Life is very hard when you're uncertain as to what we want in life. It's a decision I'll have to make on my own.

THE SIMPLE COTTAGE

I came across a train of thought that caught
me in a world of abstract imaginations

I flew over rolling hills and grand mountains expecting
to come upon a great peak I fell to my amazement

Down to a deep valley hidden
within the mountain range
Simple knowledge of its location to
all but no caring to explore it
A simple cottage plotted along the
jagged peaks of a dark valley
Passed by most to all who see it

A curiosity as a lingering dare came on my curious
heart to finally see what was within it
An expected stove, bed or two, with a boiling cauldron
Two elderly couples rocking back in forth reading
Nothing more to expect of its size and
proportion, excitement lacking, yet only wishing
to confirm my stereotypical imagination
Walking the well-planned steps as a testament
to traditional style coming to the door
expecting to see sweet old smiles

Being vacuumed across the threshold of questioning

a much larger mansion appears beyond its door

A room of many rooms of marble

floor a variety of many doors

Light encompassing the vast collection of deeper

knowledge that few have been able to behold

A library not of books and words but the

governing philosophy of man's world

I came to explore no longer consumed by

darkness but overwhelmed with light

A particular door that fascinated me that

seemed to consume light that dared its path

it lingered warning yet enticed me

Coming before its threatening aura daring to touch its

forbidden knob and turn to open what I knew of not

Daring to walk into a vast darkness

the door slamming behind me

Crossed through a threshold of what is unknown

hearing a hoarse voice behind the veils of darkness

"I am fear who dares to try to understand

me" a crackled voice breaks the air

"I am whatever horrors chase you in the

night; I am the reaper of the night"

A trembling terror gripping me helpless against

my desire for knowledge of truth to this beast

A ten-foot giant perchance with many eyes

thousands of teeth to devour me

A creature from the deepest darkest sea that

devours men for many years it might be

I could only ponder such things that I was bothered

What lay beyond the veils that hid his face so well?

As an answer to a prayer for wisdom a candle I found

Lighting itself as a means of uncontrolled

learning it pierced and tore at the veils

Revealed behind the darkness hunched

in a corner back bent by age

An old man with beady eyes shielded his

eyes with his long-crackled fingers

Chalky white skin seemed to peel from his body

a figure enclosed in the black of black

Long dirty hair almost to the floor

a coward before the light

His power only in the veils that surrounded him

His defense lied only in those who would not dare

Such a sad thing to see the creature that bore such

power I left disappointed in my failed assumption

A curious door grabbed my attention

Chains of iron and gold glomming in the light

I approached its strong presence that cried in the room

and peered at its heavy weight pushing the doors open

Quickly the pushed aside to my amazement walking

through intimidated by the scene of their strength

I saw a man of great muscle flexing

the power of his might

Beauty piercing the fabrics of time

I saw with amazement the great deeds he has done

Plastered on the wall seeming endless of

might none could bring him to his knees

Staring endlessly on the wall a great

mirror he peered in deep

A small frail figure contesting

him for proof of his deeds

Smashing the window with his fist

he cried I am perfect indeed

Seeing the fragmented mirror, he prized scattered about

with blood dripping from his arm perfection marred he

could not live with weakness he died drained of blood

never fixing least he admit to being just a little weak

Disappointed with obvious folly I walked out

seeing how the doors so easily passed entering

Hidden hinges made of wood ready to splinter and break

The next door that held me in awe stood above

the rest and proclaimed to be the best

On its either side golden statues stand in awe

welcoming to behold what lay beyond

Golden swans etched on either door

side preceded a Persian rug

Silver lining along its doors, gems etched in

perfect pattern not broken in any matter

A bold approach to see what lie in obvious

perfection led to perfect beauty

Skin so smooth and clear a form of

purity beyond recognition

Glowing long hair trimmed to perfection a silky tribute

Eyes as deep as jasper, eyelashes beckoning to come

Small red mouth appeared delicious a

buttery soft voice so enchanting

Half revealing breasts hanging

temptation started banging

Covered what need to bring guess but

revealing enough to lure attention

Mile long legs gliding shifting her stare to

draw her audience close a false interest

Many down below eyes averted sunken

behind pale skinned heads

Aging like rotten fruit left in a damp room

Wrinkled creatures that bear the mark

of death and steal the soul

Smells of death nothing left but bones they

reach in vain attempt for her gown

As she flirted she fell tripping over

an old hour glass breaking

Sand engulfing, caught amongst her

admirers slowly wrinkled and turning to

gaze upon the next queen to behold

Nothing great of such a pointless

cycle a tragedy of great weight

Leaving I see the doors from the inner side show

rust and neglect and gems broken amongst piles

of sand pouring from broken hour glasses

Their lined such a sight an outpouring

of such wealth it was a grand sight

Vast door beyond what I could perceive

a promise of joy surely it will bring

Approaching their splendor and eyeing with

greed passing through with great difficulty

Golden statues stood on either end

with golden chains in each hand

Snarling grins enjoying the sight of a small

frail man hurrying about to all ends

Chairs around neck, waist, legs, and

arms pulled by their empty promises

Piles of gold, silver, gems, and great value

heaped all about by his constant work

Just out of reach but there to see watching

as it dwindles from many thieves

Withered by the heat of his passion he passes

old photos with the contents they held

long gone and forever out of his reach

He expires naked and alone buried by heavy gold

This surely a sad existence perhaps the vainest

Leaving the room seeing the difficulty being

the piles of wealth held the doors closed

Worthless weight that drove the man alone

Coming to a simple wooden door with

no great design for beauty but curious

to find its contents I must explore

A man of no great strength or deed who

brings fear to that pale withered man

He is adventurous opening various doors

demising plans to discover the contents

of what no one had ever explored

Piece by piece he escapes narrowly only

to eventually find tragedy

Though his courage could pierce fears veil he could

not see where not fear but wisdom forbade the way

Another door I must see and implore to learn more

I came to this door of great design

flowing with such impossible design

Never before seeing its creation so complicated

I try to understand its mysterious lure

Opening by means I have not seen it reveals

huddled figures peering deep in written words

searching for hidden answers and meaning

Skeletal remains never happy with just one page

Flipping through trying to understand but

never satisfied with just one answer

Webs have grown over the riddled bodies

spiders consume them of all their gain

To be lost in darkness it's such a shame to hold

such treasures yet they are lost once again

Leaving them to rot I cross the room

the door is simpler than I thought

Back in the mansion a hollow echo

fills with trembling laughter

"All is vain all is naught who can

bring sense to worthless lots"

"Life is vain yet has hidden purpose find it

amongst such fools or forever be lost"

To find the truth to the cottage I did

not find treasure to be plundered but

merely a net of traps to betray

The very principle and very thing I never came

to find was truth in itself to know the way

A small crevice etched in the wall
nothing to draw me caught my eye

I came to peer in its long dark hall which composed a
maze of twists and turns linked doors to pits and falls

Seeking her words, I linger and
drive myself in dark halls
What I shall find only determines my means
of desiring to find her lest I fall
Will I put down selfish ways and simple answers
and make the sacrifice of all I used to believe
Is to determine what ending I shall bring

WHO AM I?

I can't quite describe how I feel other than I am not quite sure rather I am feeling anything or not. It rather seems That I am merely a shell with hollow echoes of humanity that vaguely bounce about. My memories feel as If the memories of another man. I look in the mirror and I am not quite sure who I am even looking at. My body aches all over and I feel a deep pain in my chest and back. It feels as if the vest and passion of youth has died away and only a flutter of a phantom flame distantly reminds me of shortcomings that haunt my every waking hours. Sure, I have what appears to be emotions but it only looks like anger, sadness and pain is all I left inside me. Overwhelming primitive emotions that can't quite recall why they are there. It's even as if the basic carnal instinct of lust is dulled out. I see a beautiful woman and I know I find her attractive but am not fully there. It's like looking at her through a foggy mirror. I recognize her and her beauty but can't quite take into her. I sometimes wonder if I am even human. It's more like I am waiting for death and eternal punishment for my failure to stay with God. It's like I went and hid from myself and my true self even gave up on finding myself. I convinced myself to hate love as it leads to a shattered heart and lost hopes. It's as if

my spirit is beyond broken and crushed. It's as if my soul
has long died and I am only an empty shell. I am lead
to believe that I can never love again as if my curse
of myself after the madness ensued after the crushing
realities of my life came to me. I swore a blood oath
and it bound me. There are times that if a beautiful
woman stood right before me bare naked and positioned
beautifully I would have little to no response. The
attraction is their but I simply just do not care. Not
to sound brutish or inscribe I only care for the physical
manifestation of a woman's shell but I have always loved
and appreciated the female form from an artistic sense.
May sound strange but to me it is not. I have always
loved beauty and found the female form to be very
enticing. Not so much as an attraction alone but more
of an admiration of nature. I feel as if the world has
drained me of everything. Laughter seems like when you
eat a bunch of candy on an empty stomach. I feel as if I
have no control over the madness of this world. Over
all I can say I have a sense of numbness inside as if I was
dead. At least when I had my heart broken when in love
it was not an empty feeling with primitive feelings of
hate and grief. At least I still felt love. This emptiness
has made life a struggle just to live at all.

AN ESSAY ON THE PROGRESS OF MANKIND

While I must mark the amazing distance our race has
climbed in distance from his early days in dirt ridden
caves eating the fleas off his fellow man from the
ingenuity of marking the skies with our passing and
discovering our innards and its purpose I must deny
mankind's reason to celebrate its ageless passing as we
have but become cattle to feed the wanting grass,
fattened by our well-earned rewards of the tireless
work of our ancestors barely given a thought as we
arrogantly soak in our ill gained accomplishments.
A passing thought to the moss-covered giants we
exist upon. A sullen expression as their legacies rot
in the wake of fools claiming ill gained glory. I
sought to find wisdom in my books in given praise
to the predecessors that gave us the wonder of our
modern existence but with no audience in which
to share the treasures of our founding existence,
I found such tributes to be nothing more than a
mocking masquerade of faded faces of humanities
founding intellects that gave us such rich treasures of
knowledge and yet the immortal praise left to us is left
to garner dust on rotted tombs and hardly a glance in
humanities rich history of provocative thought. I find

myself a man amongst apes barely grasping the throngs
of such powerful intellects as I seek convergence
amongst the rotted waters to catch up to my primal
counterparts least the sorrow of the ancient world's
loss leaves me in a melancholy state with no escape. The
price but the sinking light in the proverbial distance
of my mind being darkened to find complacencies in the
company of fools. Seeking freedom from the jeers of
my fellow peers for lifting the memories of long dead
men and women, responsible for searing the treasures
of our current comforts into our existence. Men such
as Galileo Galilei, Isaac Newton, Socrates, Plato,
Einstein, Gabriel Rossetti, William Hunt and many
more names whose brilliance, echoes upon the ignorant
walls of modern humanity, a deaf wall of worthless
flesh seeping into the compliance of their comforted
existence. Appraisal only of vain beauties that rot as
the rose in the never-ending reminder of carnal decay
that existence cruelly demonstrates our mortality. Our
blind ignorance never seeming to grasp the concept
that inevitable clasps upon our throats slowly denying
life till we collapse, poisoned with age and a hideous
display of our curse. A similar fate found upon the elite
of our societies, strong bodies that only come to the
ashes of our frail existence to be spread upon the wind
and lost without memory. Knowledge that contains

immortal value that can forever be passed on and built without losing its value has found mortality in the hands of ignorance. With no curious minds to embrace wisdoms lovely touch. Shall this burning flame reignite the dark fires of ignorance and leave the work of our betters to whither in forgotten tombs. Have our societies embraced the mock education social status so that the accumulated wisdom and knowledge of our ancestors be lost to fools without understanding? Shall knowledge be as a lost language to dribble on the tongues of empty minds? Shall we memorize the words of our betters without understanding and bury such discovery by dogs who ascribe our ancestors to be nothing more than superstitious cavemen afraid of the dancing shadows on walls never recalling the accomplishments of those before us? Shall we nary remember the pain staking distance they drudged to bring us where we are today? We know not but to set our minds on words repeated but we refuse to embrace the meaning behind such monuments. I am embittered at my own failings and calm composure before a sea of lunacy and delightful ignorance. A drug induced coma into the higher learning's that taught us not what exists but why, when and question the authority's stances of the majority to prove its understanding rather than blind memorized acceptance. Did not the pre-Raphaelites refuse to be carbon copies but leave their

own prints of accomplishments in the sand instead

of stepping upon the footprints of others? Did not

Galileo face the grave consequences of transgressing

the public declarations and found the facts of his days

but myths on a blurry mural? Are we to drain into the

brainwashed states of memorization and pretentious

quoting without knowing the power of the words we

speak? I am at a loss to how we may endeavor in a world

that sinks to a vegetable state and leaves us wanting

of the nectar of knowledge. A visage of a shrinking

shadow starved of curious minds probing into the

light of knowledge. Our books but a empty recital

of unknown words that bear no meaning to their

speaker. We sought to educate the world but gained

a lazy stance that left our words meaningless. Our

society hanging on the fringe of a teenage soap opera

without end. Pretending to be adults in a high school

setting we blandly coexist in. The blinding images that

bear lies to us as we stare into the pretty flashing

box informing us of reality when we have lost the

sensitivity to realities touch. We have lost our ability

to think and reason and sought answers from a box.

The sensitivity to true knowledge leaves us in a hurtful

gaze that infringes us to see in the bright of day as

we have become adjusted to the comfortable darkness

of blissful ignorance. Once again dragged to Plato's cave of deceiving shadows as the blind informs the blind of the colors of the world and their meaning. A frivolous mess of words that carry empty words across the ignorant masses. No longer do we have leaders who can ascribe the world as it truly is rather for truth or deceit but knowledge has been lost to us as a tide that retreats from the shores. Yet is hope in the return of the tide as it covers the dead, once again once the horrors of ignorance grip our species in punishment for our arrogant ascension amongst the stars? Shall the horrors of humanity once again be covered by the sea and only but a muddied visage be allowed to pierce the surface till we once again lapse back into our lethargic ways? Only time will tell our tale and shall we relive our tragic existence where the cruel lessons of life shall give us pause in our self-destructive ways.

HOPE?

This is a question rather than a statement when reflecting onto the concept that has driven human hearts for generations. I plead to seek refuge from the zombie like disease striking Americans into a state of obedient stupor following these canned definitions of hope that is no more natural than the processed cheese in a can the corpulent masses suck down with eager bellies to digest the empty words of false saviors panning out their artificial promises. No let me tell you what hope really is. First off it is not some feel good happy message to calm you into a drug induced stupor. It is not found amongst flowery fields boasting of spring infused sunshine that makes you want to sing like some narcotic fool tripping on the latest fling in the drug market. It is not some night class positivity seminar designed to separate you from your hard-earned money through giving off pretty speeches and lies about how wonderful life is. It is not some hopped up savior swooping from the sky to save us from some stereotypical villain painted by the mass media to indulge in a black in white world of the little guy getting the upper hand. It is not some design of grand victory where all is well if we just press a little harder to reach the greener grass on the other side. It is not what you have been told all your life where you desperately cling to this facade trying to make it work for you to paint on a plastic smile when you in reality feel like death has eaten you from the inside. It is not the cliché you have been fed your entire life that only sickens you deep down inside and leaves you hungry no matter how much of the social elite cram down your throat to alleviate themselves of the guilt-ridden rage that hollowed out their soul long ago. Now that I have hollowed out the masses of bull shit you have been fed about what hope is let me tell you what the real definition of hope is with a solid background as to why. Hope is the sister of truth and faith. They are not beautiful in the traditional vain American way but would rather be considered ugly abominations inflicted with the sin of mankind's divulgence in rebellion towards morality. Once beautiful in every aspect inward and outward they were marred by the fall of mankind in its attempt at self-independence and the realization of mortality, death and decay. They are cold, hard creatures to behold that wrench at the stomach and seek to empty out our bowels as they attempt to wrench out the filth we have filled ourselves with. Their embittered anger well deserved from the desecration we have heaped upon them. Truth is well founded in just morality toward our fellow man which should be

absolute rule while faith is waiting upon the healing
of mankind through evolving as a species to undertake
progress toward a better future. Now to focus on the
aspects of hope as originally intended. To understand
hope I had to reveal a brief glimpse of her sister's
faith and truth. Who am I to say such things with
arrogance? I am a fool who can reveal his sloth and
ignorance at hopes that nature who made me can save
me from this vile existence. I learned from experience
just how empty I am without my natural consciences.
Now to ascribe to what hope is without empty displays
of clichéd crap of pretty images cast in front of your
eyes like some flashing TV screen demanding you submit
to its every whim and imagination, I have to reveal that
the inner beauty that is found in hope can transform
the ugly appearance it posses'. Hope is the found in the
stars not for their light but how they pierce the eons
of darkness to reach us. Despite the fact many are long
dead, their light still reaches us for generations on
end and live on in our sight though long destroyed
to the bowels of time. It is the contrast of great evil
to a little good that always overcomes in the end no
matter how tiny the light. Though the world burns
with despair, hope is the perseverance to endure this
evil and know that there is the ability to evolve beyond
our knuckle dragging history. It is an ugly hard faucet

to hold unto but it's beautiful in accomplishing. It is the application of endurance through the black night that seeks to find its redemption amongst the bleak mountains of uncertainty that hide our destiny, our hope not in carnal man but in extension of our spirits.

Her sister faith is the tough mistress that is difficult to keep one's eyes on that deep down inside us we know the promise of redemption is nigh and that should we endure but a little longer our agony shall be rewarded.

Finally, truth, though ugly in the reflection of our reality seeks to unveil her original glory and deliver us from the ugly wrath our beginnings were exposed to, to deliver us through acknowledge the filth and disparity mankind has fallen into and emerge a new creature birthed in pain, despair and agony. Birth has never been pretty or pleasant to view. It is traumatic, it is painful, it is disgusting yet we call birth beautiful. Why? Why do we call something so disgusting, painful and miserable as birth as something beautiful? It is the accomplishment of overcoming a change of place.

It is the successful transition from utter darkness to light and the chapter of a life begun. Just because we are only physically born once does not mean we never have to endure the birthing process again. Our lives forever change and we are reborn constantly as we evolve beyond old traditions and religion that holds us hostage to paranoia and ignorance. True faith is the belief in mankind's ability to evolve beyond old traditions and embracing a world of science and progress.

LOVE POEMS

This section is devoted to stories from the heart. This reflects one my greatest muses/tormentors and that is a beautiful woman. Love, a concept that is often abused and thwarted by our sex obsessed society that thinks one-night flings are a collection of love's like small beads to string around their necks in the conquests of their redundant lifestyles that only leave them wanting more. I am not one to push extremes in relationships as I believe marriage to be a hoax and causing more problems then solving. These are from my days where I was a hopeless romantic before I learned the dirty truths to love among humans.

THE FORGE THAT BURNS COLD

My love my dear who does limber amongst my sea of
thoughts does the continence of my dreary face even
draw the slightest mercy in your most virtuous heart.
Is thine hand drawn asunder to part my voice in dreary
hate or some vow brought you far to acquire even the
slightest sigh from your fair lips?
Is the amber that burned hot in our youth grown to ice
on the cruel marble floor?
Has the warmth we shared on cold winter days a
passing thought?
What is it that our hearts once mended, melted in the
iron forge only but a pleasant dream past from memory.
The thirst that clenches my throat does choke the very
air from me and chills my blood to again hold your soft
hand.
Is fate so cruel that it mocks my plight to cast me on
high only to make your figure but a dot on a barren
world?
High esteem met with bitter dispute over fame or love is
but a trifle.
Would but a simple loving sigh, I should cast myself a
martyr to love eternally.
Such is it that you wane away with the dying world not
bearing to view its tortured cries as it bleeds the last of

life from her dried veins.

What happened as time bleed us away to lead us to only

be a simply passing of strangers in a distant land?

LOST DREAMS

Oh, woe is me whom love did grievously deny me. To feel that ilk, that sickness of the soul when the heart seeks his other side. Her gentle voice, her loving eyes, who did put a spark in my life. My uttered words I will regret until I die, the secret of my hated desire to be by her side. This was invoked with a bitter laugh and cruel denial. Rather I have never known than to incur her bitter mockery. What was precious to my very soul drove her away from me where friendship died because of that sickening desire. Whom am I but Apollo seeking the hand of Daphne who despised his love and was driven from he, her form forever transformed into a tree. As such this tree is my bitter roots in longing for what would never be. Her memory a long-tortured thought is all I may do, in honor of honest love made true. Such a pleasure it would be that I could treasure your heart without your knowledge that our time might have been forever indeed. When you wandered far from me, I wished for your company again to kindle in blissful friendship but nay my heart could not hold out and buckled from living a lie. My vow of death to the heart that betrayed, I swore an oath to kill the desire of my other and with blood did I make this unholy pact and brought death to my soul, forever consumed indeed.

SIRENS WHISPERS IN THE DARK

My mistress calls me, she beckons my doom,

Her gentle call does lap over my heart,

Smooth foam tipped fingers on a rocky shore,

Her most gentle touch where my soul does loom.

Yet this love without dispute would bear lies,

Quick her rage does grow, her anger so cold,

Bearing down on wary mortal souls consuming,

Although our creation be two opposed,

This sweet union could not lie beyond hope,

Our affair adores earth with gentle slopes,

Dressed neatly least her belly lie exposed.

THE UNNAMED LULLABY

As I lay my tired head upon your tender breasts, I listen
to your hearts lovely lullaby, sweet breaths rising slowly
up and down, your gentle sighs an ode to beauties melody.
Soft warm flesh as velvet sheets subtle pulse keeps your
beat, soft spoken words give tribute to the muse's song
to hear your lovely thoughts. Precious gems hold no
sparkle compared to your windows emerald gleam, no
vacancy but kindness dwells within. The shine of hair,
the youthful face, the softest touch, thine tender kiss,
most fine-tuned song, none compare or stand so fair to
the beauty of life within.

SONNET 1 (THE JOURNEY OF ORPHEUS)

O tis the day I fall among dead ways

May it be known; love be as the undead;

O tis the sad truth to bury the dread.

O tis the hour mine heart shall surely pay,

Again, to mourn where mine salted, tears lead.

Whom should foretell that I should be easy game?

Cupid's heinous lead arrow, surely, I'm slain,

Where mine heart wondered, where

dreams forever bleed.

Sever thine tongue, o wretch, o wicked sway,

Held many a rose, never pricked a finger,

Hand hath not felt burn of love's most holy beacon.

Rather I die a thousand deaths a day,

Then live in a thousand loves eternally,

A burning hell of passions internally.

WHAT I REALLY LOST

Caught in a state of tangent dreams,

Ensnared by a web of dreaded realities.

Holding tight, refusing to let go.

Controlling fate stole my choice least I expire.

A thin wire snaps releasing heavy bags of lovely grief.

Weakened limb hang as a drained tree

Her face plunging down a darkened path,

fading into forgotten lands

Seeing her dissipate as a distant memory

Left with her whipping garment in

my hand, my only memory

Heavy bags gone so fast, tense pain

released such joyful sorrow in me

Wondering where I am in this place of

forgotten hopes and dreams

Losing sight of my reach, finding paths never breached

SUNSHINE

I will be your wood if you be my fire

I will be your mouth if you be my voice

I will be your sword if you be my sheath

I will be your arrow if you be my bow

I will be your bread if you be my butter

I will be your bread if you be my butter

I will be your mountain if you be my peak

I will be your forest if you be my shade

I will be your desire if you be my dream

I will be your sunset if you be my sunrise

I will be your stars if you be my night

I will be your clouds if you be my sky

I will be your moonlight if you be my sunshine

Always remember that for the moon to shine he needs

his sunshine.

JUST ANOTHER LOVE POEM

I came across such a field, with bent wheat tearing its
yield
Stars shot across the sky where my maker left me to die
To hold this place amongst the dead, the land of where
blood remains yet unshed
Trail I followed to get hear is not where I was headed
Could not find heaven's scent where decay followed
The beating heart of mistaken hollow... drums my
forsaken approach
Built on the fringe of where good men lie avenged
Nurtured ground with life's cold bitter edge
Thin sliced smiles, leaking love, seeping down my teary
paths
I could not hold the ropes to my savior's heels, now I
plummet amongst the dead
His ever-loving face fading... fading in forgetting mists
Another chapter closed with bitter damp hand
Now I hold this gun of truth to my head
That hope is lost... which was forever in my grasp but
without my hand
My breadcrumbs to lead where I dwelt are crimson
beware
Find them before they perish in the dust follow not
where emotions betray the Holy Ghost

Oh, Judas that I should find you withered in this crypt

Where the unforgiving murders lie... I lay my head to

wait for the removing of my head

The God I loved shall be the God who deals my final blow

This I brought upon myself... I follower of heart is my

crime... My end is near

SHATTERED SURFACES

I once held you in my dreams

We danced under silken strands of milky moonlight

Over the mirrored reflection of a bottomless lake

Nothing could have severed those cords that held us

in this dream

Like all dreams, it did fade

A thousand suns, of bright optimistic rays left their

mark

I now stand in the crackled remains of a lake's grave;

wondering where it came from

Nothing comes to mind of bounding strength; only

the thin cords of distant memory

I remember when you did no wrong

Purity seemed as close as the enwrapping air

Freedom was your suitor, who bid you good day

You held a golden script of blameless words

I remember seeing you bent down over burdened with

some invisible weight

You were wrapped in the shadows of a decayed past

I could hear the chains rattle as you slumped in prison

shade

The words you spoke rusted the proclamation to life

and truth

Mirrors lie to us every day

They tell us who we are so we will feel safe

I held you once over that mirrored lake

What is the point to dreaming of lies; in the end it

only makes us want to go hide

I think each reflection I see tells the truth by speaking

that which is not true

The shattered lines of that plane remind us of how

insecure we are

I pushed you away because I could not see

I dream to satisfy the hunger of that which can never

be; then I move on unashamed

STRONG DESIRES (THE ORIGINAL)

I am captivated by such a work of art

that is before my wanting eyes

I see a piece that God surely prized

A woman of great design

A swan that glides over the dark crystal lake of

endless horizon is nothing as smooth as your smile

Hair that flows for endless miles

I want to gaze deep into the pools of your

eyes, to dive into its purest place

Can the Sapphire burn as bright?

Can the ocean reach your depths?

Can the eagles cry ascend to your heights?

Can the diamond pierce your soul?

Can the wind compete with your steps?

The song on my lips is your kiss

The voice that is the soothing

rain upon the famine land

To touch my tongue with honey is to

feel your sweet hands grasp

The light of my day is from your shine

The hottest fire could not consume the passion

that lies within the dark chambers of my heart

The stars are but blunt marbles compared

to the honor of your glare

I could compass all the days to see watch

you in the depths of your slumber

To hold such an eternal treasure is

the dreams of lost kings of old

Even when time attempts to eat at you, he cannot

deny your splendor that is proclaimed at this time

To gain your love is as the moon so

beautiful, yet always beyond my touch

Alas love is a cruel Mistress that sits before

me as I reach for her as a thirsty prisoner,

yet I am yet to grasp her gentle finger

The simple pleasure of knowing your grandeur is

the drive that keeps me hoping for another.

STRONG DESIRES
(THE REMAKE)

I am captivated by such a work that

is before my wanting eyes

I see a piece that God must surely

prize, a woman of great design

Hair that flows for endless miles

I want to gaze deep into the pools of your eyes

Can the sapphire burn as bright?

Can the ocean reach your depths?

Can the eagles cry ascend to your heights?

Can the diamond pierce your soul?

To hold such an eternal treasure is

the dreams of lost kings of old

To touch my tongue with honey is to

feel your sweet hands grasp

Can the wind compete with your steps?

The song on my lips is your kiss

The voice that is the soothing

rain upon the famine land

I could compass all the days to watch

you in the depths of your slumber

The light of my day is from your shine

THAWING

Eternal sunshine upon the frozen
walls of my hollow heart
Thaws out my contempt for love embraces
the prisoner waiting within
Thine beauty being as the magnified crystal
perfected in time and pressure within
Blessed heart of gold, song of the beloved dove
whose power brings the dark captive home
The dark flames of betrayal quenched with this
passionate love that holds eternal life within
The shifting sands of timeless dreams
casting hopes for this desired treasure
Deep within the pool of forgotten woes, her
warm embrace melts the ice that holds me cold
Barren bitter lips transformed by her gentle kiss
Tears of cleansing and flowing power
hold tight to her sacred face
Her pure white flower making a world gone
astray cry a hope of innocence being redeemed
Can anyone hold true to stand before her soft
eyes that beg of love to fill our hearts?
In which modesty comes to play, for she knows her well
Soothing words as the April winds that
warm the frozen winter grounds

The ocean's depths could not bury thine

worth to this light forsaken world

A swan's grace is as the rocks of broken ground

compared to the swift flow of your holy tread

Can the heart contain such love that seeps

from your unending wells of love?

Nay I say but it bursts over upon surrounding flowers

dried and wilted for want of this nourishment that

brings reason to life's blood that seems to pose as venom

Oh, darkness flees you have no hold for the

light of this loving creature that holds

truth to the legend of a virtuous woman

Death bow your head in dishonor upon this day for

your desire is lost and her love I shall forever acquire

The flame is lit, who shall challenge its healing power

WINTERS ADVOCATE

Snow white snow bright newlyweds you be tonight

To tell a tale we must go back to where you first were

made lovestruck

Foolish bird that sings you songs; though you looked

toward another eye were set straight to the coming

one

The invasion was short and quick to your heart you

stood no chance beauty bound your love

Broken gates open wide; your heart left to plunder she

took her place deep within

Come young man and woman, your ways shall embrace,

your flesh becomes one, yet shall you mold to summer's

song?

Nay, I say to this folly, let summer rest, for she is weary

The fruit of love birthed in summer is merle left to rot

in the sun for lust is the concept of her game short and

sweet but never long

Yet be winter's advocate who testifies to true long-

lasting love

Ice shall preserve this is never wrong cold and harsh

yet pure and true be forever new

Be as the snow high in the mountaintops never touched

nor corrupted but pure white blankets

Her harsh blowing winds will testify of your trials, yet

though snow only grows closer, stronger and harder: a

shield that cannot break

Oh, woman of gentle touch place upon ye her garments,

be the tempest of winter whose beauty and splendor that

could blush the moon had she blood

Oh man of faith be strong and harsh to those who

come to take your prize

Fierce is winter's howl hard is her blow take to

strength all this you know

Let them join together embrace tight, snow white snow

bright newlyweds you be tonight keep this tale deep in

heart become winters advocate to keep the fight

Hand and hand, you tread the road where you go

nobody knows

PRETENDING TO BE IN LOVE

I met a woman today or rather a menace towards my content countenance that ravaged at my well-crafted solitude I rather came to enjoy. Rather than bask in the blissful void of shadows contemplating the finer things of our contradictory existence I found myself conjuring her wrathful presence in that private spot in the deep recesses of my mind. That lovely chaos that beheld my fancy and took captive a force within I thought I had lost.

Her eyes deep blue beams of light that sting with a cold hard steel that pierces liken to a vengeful dagger borrowing into what's left of my tattered soul. A smile that mockingly follows me under the cool blue moon burning her glare into my mind like some tacky clichéd tattoo that begs attention. Midnight black hair that seers the very fabric of my attention commanding my every thought yet why can I not purge this perfection of feminine art from my mind. Why can I not pry my thoughts from her every breath and steady heartbeat. Remove yourself from my heart you viper, naught but a shrapnel shrouded amidst the fleshy cage you sought intrusion. Leave to my musings and take those cold blue pools that glare from my sight. Take the glossy midnight black hair away that bears heavy on my soul.

Let not the lips cold pressed seek my attention by drive
thy harpy enchantment from this place. Let my mind
be free and clean that you may not invade my abysmal
thoughts. Thy shadow cast upon the bleak wall a curse
to the visage that deters sleep to bring rest along. You
are there to come for my peace! A tyrant to rule my
nights with the disease called love!
Demon leaves me to wallow alone and take thine
claws out from my soul. Possess another or be driven
to the pigs to carry those cold blue eyes amidst
the unforgiving seas that I never again shall have
perfection beheld. Your love be a curse to seek I know
from the vain noble cause. The very journey that drives
my sex to endless madness in lust filled pursuit. Only
through this dream of companionship and pursuit can
I know that I am truly alive yet no greater pain than
to accept my mistress called desire to know I yet breath.
Only left to wait her passing and suffer anew.

THE LOVE SHADOW

My heart aches every night with untold agony at
your shadowed sight. I dream of you every waking
hour, breath caught in a snare with no release to
my tortured thoughts. These clichéd thoughts and
feelings a quagmire of my delusions. This is the enigma
of my shattered conscious. I cannot feel but the subtle
whisper of your tender voice, the cruel silence that
follows your blessed song. The burning passion as I
feel the warmth of your life force flowing beneath my
wanting fingertips. The breath slipping past my lips in
a cool fiery embrace. The seductive giggle that sears
my soul in iron clad place. I don't know your name. I
don't even know where I meet you. I don't know the
tone of your silky flesh nor do I really care. I don't
know the color of your hair or the way the sun shines
through your silken strands. I don't know the shade of
your eyes. Rather they gleam of emerald hues begotten
of rolling seas. Perhaps the endless blue losing me in
gentle flight in pure skies. Should they bear earthy
brown strong and proud. Maybe the purest silver gray
reflecting the pure soul of heavenly display. Who
knows but perchance the colors are of multi display all
about the light and angle the catch on fire paved skies
rich with heaven's delight just in the summers eve of

a crescent moon. Her gentle smile on your subtle grin matching the star filled sky oh how the night reflects this perfect sight. How the beams gently pour down your slender form with the deepest gaze that holds me with the beat of your lively pulse. How the burning blush tears at my every thought and holds me to behold creations greatest touch. Yet I don't know any but a shadow of a wanting thought. A dream masqueraded by a God given plot. I only know this empty spot. Why I ask that I seek a woman I know not exists to complete that which was so cruelly taken in man's beginning and to time lost. The gaping hole in my heart where my female half remains lost to my touch. How can a man ever find peace when he seeks his completion in shadows cast across the blank wall and dreams of a softer song? Where lips are barren to eternal want and u simply do not know how to love but only want.

FORBIDDEN LOVE

A glimpse of light reflected off the purest eyes. The
wisps of wind that bear your silken hair, a molten
river of blissful delight. The whimsical laughter that
held darkness at bay, Apollo's heavenly bane. The silken
strands of your lips bearing heavy on my earthy mind.
The sun's fire paved skies could not touch the extent
this hellish passion no soul could deny. I stood at
the gates of my desire, denied by the simplest vow that
held us apart. The vows I sought to bear upon my lips
and seek the bond that could entangle two lives was
stolen ungracefully from me. This forbidden passion
bears the cocktail of delicious poison. The desire feels
as a thousand joys all buy tearing at my soul. Never
a greater contrast then this demonic concoction of
lust and desire born through devoted love. Many a
night I held you yet you knew not my presence till you
melted from my grasp and slumber betrayed my heart and
trust and hope became my tormentor. Though I sought
to know you it is a vain journey as another stole my
plunder. Doomed to wander the deserts ends driven
mad by every thought by heavens fallen angel. I am but
the dove without my olive branch. Shall I fall upon
this facade and seek relief in another? Shall I paint
a plastic smile with a desperate soul seeking just any

other? Rather I bear Orpheus's oath to bear my hate of cupid's arrows and devour the cruel fate to pierce my heart with the wretched lead arrow. To hold this forbidden love as heaven's bane. Oh, Orpheus shall my severed head float down the rivers of fate with barren lips, a song still mockingly seeping from their parched state? No longer to hold even a candle to light my way to holy unions state. To risk the path most souls travel or brave the lonely way the path so few bare. Destiny has had her gluttony of painful rage to hold at bay to souls an eternity away. Driven in exile from this land to never lay my eyes on the heart that is forbidden that my soul feels driven. To be as Oedipus drove unjustly insane whose eyes were punished for an ignorant crime rather I join in blindsight to never lay my eyes on the one whose love I fell pray. Never shall I forsake my heart's desire but honor demands my love of this soul remain chase for my loves purity's sake.

SPIRITUAL

This is from a time from my religious days in which I sought to emanate the kindness of Jesus Christ. I have always sought to try and be the best person I can be and now I need no excuse other than it being the right thing to do. I know now to not put my faith in one single belief system and morality is subjective to the individual but for art's sake I keep these and also, as a reminder as a part of my earlier life. I no longer hold to such draconian spirituality and realize that the God I worshiped has no definition except by what man gives God his definition which is why all gods have human characteristics.

SONNET 2 (DOVE WITHOUT AN OLIVE BRANCH)

O Mine heart oh lord, is tattered and torn,

Lead to the brink of hell's lips I sinketh.

Fought mine wars, battles hard, left in tears pink,

From mingled blood and water, mine soul mourns.

Valor echoed not from such tall tree tops,

But called the rain of such bitter defeat,

Silent drops ; mine heart poured out where I meet,

Such great pools of endless fate, I cast not.

O shall mine eyes look down ever so lonely,

Shall I fly, a dove with no olive branch,

Neither find mine place among broken reeds,

Mine reflection my only company.

Yet mine heart shall take company with such,

A man whom held burdens I felt light touch.

LORD OF THE BROKEN

Lord as I stumble across the barren fields, I sought
food to bear me through. When none could be found
I sought water for the parched throat, alas there was
none. I cried to the heaven for blessed rain but not
until I bent my knee did I find paradise at hells gate.
My wounds would not seal till my heart was given to
you. Jesus, you are my sustenance where mankind failed.
I knew no peace in this lands tyranny until you picked
me up broken and bruised. Though the stars may bear
hope for the hour, your embrace is joy's renewal. I am
weak and yet you called out to me. A sinner seeking
redemptions peace. Though the enemy seeks to devour
your rod and spear does close the lion's mouth. You
soothe the raging fire and fill your strength in the
empty vessel. You are the hope where there is no hope
and where man should surely fall. The anvil and
hammer that molds us all. Glory to heaven's king, Jesus
shall rule an army of those once called weak.

ALTAR OF TEARS

I left a tear on your altar. Part of me wanted to wipe it clean, the human part of me. Something inside me told me no and I could not help but compel. A simple tiny pool of grief birthed from pain. A glimpse into the heart left from God's touch of a tender soul. If you know where to look there's a story in that tear. A deep-rooted connection to the very soul it bleeds from. When we weep we shed a small amount of our essence in the droplet of water. Rather from the simple cut or bruise to the very depths of human suffering it all contains great power. I left my tear on that summer night as an offer of my own soul. I left with you a part of myself to heavy for my soul to bear. You took my pain as offering and bring comfort to the wounds I simply cannot bear. When I could not stand in my darkest hour, and my soul bleed openly part of me died with dark words uttering my greatest fears. When I could not stand and the mark of shame on my left forearm left me shamed. You held me and did collect the pain. Love is cruel in human hands. Greedy and manipulative, all to sooth the fleshes rot. Only can I be spared from the bitter blade of eternal regrets. When in my lowest state you took my broken frame so weak and held me. You took what was broken to remake me. Those who are strong are so far from you who refuse to be broken and renewed. How

God came to love the broken and shackled for only they knew the need for change. Broken hearts drained of pride where God can fill them whole and renew. Growth is pain and pain seeps from our very tears. What I left at that altar was growth of the soul through shedding of the old so I may be made renewed.

FINDING MYSELF IN ETERNITY

I often go to this place where it's just me and yet I am outside myself. In a world that makes much more sense in terms of what I see. The world is but an enclosed space of miles upon miles of landscape that stretches as a road. I am in a journey but the path is clear, concise and laid out. My strengths and weaknesses played out in simple stats and my ultimate goal is clear and simple. To find my way past obstacles to a place of rest. A one direction path with rewards to reap along the path.

Then I remember dreaming of flying. The thrill of flight, fear and adrenaline. In my youth I used to dream often. Sometimes as I lay looking up at the stars feeling as if I were going to be sucked into eternity. As if I were waiting for my God, my savior would pluck me from this tired old world. This both scared me and thrilled me deeply. Always on those long trips from California to TX. That big empty vast universe was like peering into God's very face leaving me catatonic and small, yet such gentle hands wrapping about me. I guess God loves to send us into a state of great contrast to see just how vast reality stretches beyond our understanding while feeling the gentle tugs of God that shows he is always keeping watch over us so we might understand the vast scope of his eternal power. That's when I realize just how simple minded I really am in the grand scope of creation. God never ceases to amaze me in his strange ways he has established with mankind. He always knows just what to say or reveal to astound us as we get a subtle glimpse into his ever-shifting personality. It is not that God changes but we do as a people. God just looks for the best way to approach man. Man is always changing, so God always meets us in new and exciting ways. I often feel like a 2-dimensional body trying to live in a 3d world. God always seems to know how to liberate me from the shackles of simplistic desires. A man is as free as his mind's capacity allows for him to travel.

Rather we find the very hidden spots of Earth or wither away in contempt for the cage we dwell within.

All is vanity in the end.

PROMISE

The promise of God is always true

It will never fade or lose

It stands at the door knocking

I just need to open the door

God does not lie, God does not cheat, God does not

play around

The desires we have are formerly his and he promises us a

crown

SLEEPWALKING IN GOD

Lord I walked the jagged lands. Where I held my
heart, shadows followed till your light burned
them dim. I sought you amongst the ruins where my
soul forever bleeds till you found me a broken man. I
prayed for relief but instead you taught me to stand
amongst the he graves where my Ruined body was laid
to rest you brought me to a promised land. Drew
me from great seas of sorrow removed the leaden
pellets from my heart. You birthed me once again
anew. You are the only cure for this endless hate
that delivers to a godly fate. This fire burns eternal
and thank God's mercy that forgave my slumber.

WEARY SOUL

Mine heart doth cry amongst rocks oh lord,

Mine soul doth seep in bitter tears,

Mine way has come astray and I have lost hope,

Mine days are numbered as I count mine transgressions.

I have fallen amongst shadows and mine enemies

mock me,

I beg for relief for but a moment, yet they taunt my

pleas.

I panteth after water in this dry place, yet none touch

my weary tongue,

I crawl on such scarred knees dreaming of relief.

Lord my heart does lie sore from sweet memories,

How mine songs would struggle to reach your ears,

When all had brought evil to me, how I would sing

your praises,

Such great battles won in your most holy name.

Mine tears do water such ground, may such springs

bring life to this place,

Mine cries do echo on such canyon walls in hope you

shall hear my begging,

Mine blood leads to where I had fallen, a soaked path

of grief filled regret,

Mine eyes cast down in shame, that I may not see your

disappointment.

I am a fool, who has lost himself to wonder this place,

I ran from your healing as a sacred lamb does his

medicine,

I hid that you may not find me in such disgrace yet the

blackest night holds no bars from your sight,

I now tremble before you awaiting judgment from your

righteous hand.

Now I curl in bitter pain from the scars of my fleeing,

Mine sins do mock me in this state, they laugh at my

discouragement,

I am a mockery to be found in such glorious sight,

I am poked and prodded liken to the dumb animal in a

simple cage.

But you oh Lord remember those long cold nights I

sung to you,

Your heart hath not forgotten the struggled words

to reach your throne,

How you held me shaking in the womb of darkness,

when I was all alone,

This does impart gladness in me, how you did hold my

sapphire tears in your open palm,

How you sung me to sleep when evil came to steal my

soul.

This I remember lord, how you do hold the weak and

the oppressed,

How you whisper promises of deliverance from their

hateful captors,

How you impart vengeance on the wicked in their time

of judgment,

How you give reward to your just and faithful.

Your kindness is as the sweet nectar on a bitter tongue,

Your grace is as the soothing balm on bruised hips,

Your mercy is as cool water for a dry throat,

Your strength is as bandages on an open wound.

Lord my only hope, your presences is mine only song,

Lord my only answer, your praise is my only words,

Lord my only desire, your walk is my only way,

Lord my only faith, your breath is my only relief.

Take such bitter wounds that exalt itself against you

and cast them to endless seas,

Take mine faults and cover them with your

forgetfulness,

Take mine wicked sins and bury them deep in the darkest

earth,

Take mine wounds and relieve them with your precious

blood that you may be in me.

Let a new song be born from my heart,

Let a new dance spring from my weary bones,

Let a new praise, be shouted from the rooftops,

Let a new day bring you glory in my wake.

MOONLIGHT

I am not a creator of light, but a
reflector of the sun's glory
I am the moon that hangs high in the dark
long night in a world gone astray
That light of beauty cascading upon
the world showing hope of day
Let not the tides of changing time
forget me to forever shine
This light that so radiates looms the
path of faith for a brighter day

Lifted high in my ways, I have no glory but receive
my rays from that eternal source that burns hot
all the day despite how he hides for but a time
that I should be illuminated as a softer glow of
rays of truth that won't leave a holy burn

IN NEED OF GPS (GOD'S POSITIONING SERVICE)

I am lost in a fog I seek to know the secret way. A time where the way was not enshrouded with doubt and your talks brought the kindest truth. When I burned to know your every place and the shadows bent to your every whim. The enigma where my faith was lost I sought to find myself in your holy place I endeared the elements that held your essence and came to fill my soul with your eternal breath forgive my worried heart and bleak mind that wandered from the oasis of your blessed touch I seek to place myself a cactus saturated with the nectar of God amongst a land in sinful drought Lord let your light overflow and no thirst to those in doubt.

NEVER ENDING SEARCH

I searched near and far, I have inquired of the
best, I have looked for so long, yet I never could
find the treasure that I burned for to give you
I long have looked and long desired to
find that thing of my heart's desire
I looked to the east, yet I found no peace
I pursued the west, yet I found dust
I traveled to the north, yet this
did not end that search

I journeyed to the south, yet met only a dead end
I dived in the ocean's depth, yet in all its
treasure it did not hide what I sought for
I climbed the mountain peak, yet it
held nothing in its grasps

I endured the barren desert, yet my thirst was left dry

I embraced the arctic on the frozen
river, yet it left me cold
I looked to fire, yet it only burned me
I looked to the ice, yet it held in its
frozen depths no such secret
I asked the wind in her travels, yet

she was just a clueless as I

I went to the water yet, he knew no such depth

I ran the fields, yet they were empty

I explored the dark forest, yet it

was barren of this truth

I asked the moon, yet she said she saw no such sight

I addressed the sun, yet he in all

his time could not respond

I examined the starry sky, yet though it was

endless it could not contain what I asked for

I walked the deep caverns, yet they only sang of time

I inquired the wise, yet they were as fools

I asked of the simple, yet they could not ponder

I searched the dark valley for this mystery, yet

none could be found in its dark secrets

I looked to the light, and its entire splendor,

yet even in all its power it was insufficient

I went to the gates of hell to ask the prisoners,

yet they knew nothing, but vanity

I traveled to the pearl gates of heaven, yet

I was turned around with no response

I cried in contempt, because I could not find one

word that was worthy to call upon your name

No poem, or sonnet, or song could

announce you in all of heaven's glory

Nothing could endure you; nothing

can be made to fit your throne

Lord I tried so hard, yet nothing could be found,

I have failed to find a limit to your highest praise

For it is true words can't come close to fit you

Lord all man, all creation, all the universe bows to you

WOULD YOU?

As I sit in my dark apartment room, as the
shadows of forgotten times seem to loom
Dark and secret questions began to
whisper within my eager ears

They whisper within the depths of my soul the
echo eternally in within a bleak mind
As I sit upon the bed with these dark secrets
I cry with great anguish and seem to die
The lord comes upon my presence and asks me why
With tears flowing down my face I proclaim
those question that lurked within my mind
Lord should I fall on my face a million
times would you still embrace?
Lord should I make myself a fool
would you still call me Friend?
Lord should I fail day by day would
you still hold me tight?
Lord should I stumble all the way
would you still walk by my side?
Lord should I bring you shame
would you still lift me high?
Lord should I be the worst of them
all would you still love me?

Lord surely, I have done all these things

and profess to be them all.

How should one so great hold on to

someone as me who is small?

Then the Lord said with a gentle voice.

My son did I die in vain?

BREATH

Paths along shadows lined with black roses I fall

Holding the hem of breath

A veil of thin dress wafting in the winds of thought

Trimmed icy dressing of time lining frigid dressings of
time

Book holding life's sacred secrets; the judge, the jury I
choose

Whether passing black or pearl determines home

Either place I go you lie in wait to behold

Where I walk or cry depends where my heart will lie

Gold or fire will embrace my feet that feared night

Smoke and light compete to find what my eyes shall
behold in their sight

Tongue shall meet either bitter or sweet

Visions that haunt my dream are the results of what
father time bleeds

THE GREAT DIVIDE

I awake to see a great green meadow that

proclaims peace beyond eternities dream

I walk upon the sweet scent of spring wafting

my spirit above the heights of clouds

I look around upon the land so full of lush life

I am lifted by a man I came to know as Christ

We danced about in the frolic of this paradise

We ran through the swift forest

of forgetfulness and peace

I look upon the soft glow of the humble

moon enveloping me in its wake

The soft glow of it shines a light of love

and hope upon his gentle face

As I look upon this beauty all seems to change

The night grows dark, the moon grows faint

All seems to fade in this dark hour of hopeless fate

Darkness seems to sweep upon the land and the wave of

destruction comes to push me to the cold hard ground

I see it like a wave of fire come to consume this dream

I fall to my knees to see my filth and wounds so deep

I look about in despair just to see chaos in its wake

Fire flies about in a swirl of utter defeat

I scramble for cover from its dooming fate

This is a land of pain and misery

It's a land where evil reigns and there is no peace

It burns without content and

consumes hope without mercy

I fall to my knees in these black chains

This always seems to be my defeat

Demon games, eternal shame engulf

me in its shattering reality

The laughter of my defeat echoes

through my tormented mind

The ground is as black and hard as the

heart of him who holds my chains

His scorn is like the icy knife that pierced

my heart for what seemed eternity

I cry out to that sweet face that swept me off my feet

I scream for his sweet release

I look beyond the horizon of death

to see the glimpse of light

I light that pierces the darkness it

rushes to my aid in this dark hour

It breaks me free from the chains of vanity

It leaves gifts and urges me to fight this

fierce battle and overcome deaths plight

A sword is given, a shield is made

I am wrapped in strong armor that bears a heavy weight

I strive again with a will to fight for that

paradise, so that I might cross the great

divide and live that dream once again

HUNTING MYSELF

I look to the faded way in which I came by. I seek to know and understand why I made the decisions that brought me through this valley. I cannot fathom the mind that brought me this way as the mind that sought resolution came to be from empty wondering to escape wounds that only bleed.

Seared with fire, numb with dread. I stopped feeling and never healed that speed my fall upon rocky ground and only made the wounds worse to bear. The mind that sought these methods long faded from view and my resolve birthed and renewed to lead my spirit on a different path. I wish I could say I took the path less traveled or even that I took a path at all, yet I made a path through thorns and thistles seeking an alternative to devotion to one way. Skewed on a pike of indifference to life's unjust choices. Hell bent on the one end delving down into the abyss of human error. Heaven bound on the rocky slopes spiraling upward in thick hewn clouds thundering bleak frowns from heaven bearing down hard rain and pelted with cruel hail all till we venture beyond the black veils full I doubt and worry to face the sun's harsh judgment. Hardening our countenance to bear the weight of trials. The goal to bear the cliffs of heavens challenged the path I created a stumbling fall on rocks on the lip

of the abyss I sought to circumvent. A time to resolve

my climb to the harder trail and try once more to

bear the weight and seek the journey's end and find

resolution in the king of the peaks loving mercies.

A LESSON FROM NATURE

I sit on the meadow by the river bank

She speaks to me in riddles and soft

under tones.

Her subtle whisper in the cool embrace of night

comforts me.

She tells me of long travels of seasons births and deaths

How she swells with pride in springs touch

How summer brings warmth to her clear waters to make

the sky cry

How autumn decorates her long flowing body with

many colors so kind

How the winter freezes her in awe of what will give

birth in purity to her pride

Why do you sulk, your tears cannot fill my banks as

rain water

I look with a sorrow filled heart and speak of my loss of

a kind friend

How the gentle laughter and kind smiles have departed

forever

I speak of fond memories that have passed as foggy haze

I reminisce over a friend I held dear

I don't understand in your constant life, how you

witness life and death with equal beauty never amiss

How you forever flow eternal you live and claim in

your soul you understand man's peril

Your question though well thought out in natural

observance

I flow in essence and wisdom forever with love simply

not in understanding but with no other thought

Put here by design to meet needs, through observation I

have learned much indeed

I cannot but follow the trail laid bare before my feet

Though the trail is treacherous and hard at times of

the year

I cannot change the grand will, so with patience and

good will I follow through as happy as I may

Though I grumble and complain in my fierce travels it is

those moments when I know the rocks keep me clear

Though the falls in grand splendor lack no harshness

at all,

I remember the depths the fall lead me in tears

Though beauty be found in these places always let your

heart recall,

The harsh truth of what you went through to see it

all

Therefore, in death and turmoil life is born

No difference says I in that death births beauty

But let your soul take rest in matters at hand, the

spirit of life shall death never lay his hands

In this, know that love shall forever bound, that in
this his soul shall ever live in your heart always and
forever so be sound.

THE MODERN PRODIGAL

A chasm to chase my thoughts, a mouth to swallow
the indignities of human error amongst swollen glands
pierced with silent cries in a distant faded meadow. The
grave weeps for comfort never found amongst unknown
ruins. Bearing witness to hells lips so gently wrapping
the suckled breasts of time. Proclaim all you grey souls
whimpering on the edge of the prodigal son's return
to break us free. A place to fold our hands and feed
the hungry ground. His return a myth amongst cruel
lies that burn marks on our broken bodies. Before me
I saw lying amongst mankind's ruins a child amongst
the spoils of wars wrought by ignorance in her prime.
Behold he lies before us the spectacle of idol minds. His
eyes long removed to cease beauties loves. His ears are
stuffed with false dreams stripped by men whose only
desire is to consume. His hands removed that he should
not feel his way to freedom. His nose removed that
flowers cease to encourage. His tongue stripped least
justice hear his pleas. His smile filled with broken teeth,
an inverted frown that the cruel hands that bound
him might spare his bruised face. His name well known
and long forsaken is innocence but long forgotten as
he lies amongst rotting tombs so far away.

BROKEN ART DISPLAYS IN THE SKY

I look to the sky and behold nature's grand expression on display. Grey clouds reaching high into the sky as if arms stretched from the earth. Her cry to receive escape from man's hell-bent foundation. Their watery eyes stretched far in desperation to be free. In time heaven will weep in sight of mother earth's plight and shall reign the wrath of her hatred of man's godless fate. In a time of cleansing death shall sing for his bounty and mother earth shall sing of relief.

A single strand of rainbow colors caught in the sky. The darkened eyes bear her sight against the sun's luminous glow. Struggling in her wake connected not by ground or sky but standing against harsh sunlight and just beyond the darkness that must approach. Slowly faded partly colored she shows. Do you princess of the sky offer but a gleam of hope. Perhaps a small glimpse of beauty in a harsh bright world always threatened with glom. Fading softly in the darkening blue but still warm in my memory. is your plight simply a kind word to the weary soul? Though broken you stand tall in the sky. Slowly fading but only for a time until nature again lets you glow. Fade sweet colors in kind words of farewell eager I await your return that I may have your sweet kiss bestowed.

GRANDPA

A strong soldier that knew not defeat
A man tough as nails, but a heart as soft as gold
Fought for our nation and rights
that we hold on to tight

He stood strong throughout the fight in the night

Seen bullets fly, and men die
Seen the carnage that war brings
Few know the horrors

The lord's light brought him through that fight

A man of valor
I wonder at times how it was
To fight that monster
Lived through those dreaded times
Lived through the fear of the Cold war
Witnessed the fall of the red monster
Seen lives come and go
Seen many things change

Heard our nation's cry upon that perilous day
That the murder came and destroyed

our proudest towers

Hear lays a man who achieved great honor

A hero not forgotten
I will miss you grandpa

FENCE SITTING

I cast my lot on greener grass, but the secure hard
rocks did gain my glance,
Though the soft grass embraced my feet with such a
cool touch, the tendril bit deep into my ankles with a
barbed touch.
Fetters that held tight and constricted veins and
blood, I lost my freedom for a softer touch.
I sought the rocks though they burned hot, they
secured me though it pained to impinge my feet,
Though I lingered on the edge of contrasts from time
to time, nothing hurt greater than the iron cast
fence.
Impaled on solid iron the tendrils did reach, the
burning conviction seared not far from my reach,
Though one me seek to think the best of both worlds is
the dream, it is the nightmare of consequences that the
soul must endear.
Burning conviction and cruel addictions brought me
quickly to my knees, I sought the pleasure of softer
ground and security from the vile tendrils and only
found myself impaled on the fence I sought to cradle.
I cannot run from the drag of life's unfair pitches but
seeking comfort in mindless addictions left my wanting
something more.

Better to burn on the hot coals of Godly conviction

then seek relief on greener grounds.

No better revelation than to see the toxic

representation and no greater fool than to seek both

on a barrier that bears the ill tides of flip flopping

sensations.

Though the thrill be but a season, the eternal

condemnation is a price none can afford for such a

mediocre existence.

I impaled my heart on a fence and now I must endear

God's greater conviction with searing agony but never

again shall I bear the nectar of life's kinder sensations.

Only time shall tell how great God's mercy shall impart

on me despite my foolish temptations.

THE CANVAS WE POUR OURSELVES ONTO

I look upon a bleak land in which I traveled. The bumps
and rough edges that dragged the life from me in
thin red stripes that painted the land with suffering.
I looked to dark depths my heart dragged me and saw
the broken earth from where my dirt clogged body
emerged in pocketed places. From whence holes did
dot now small mounds do rise in remembrance of this
timeframe. I held to my blanketed stare to behold the
canvas did create and through it all the art was in
the prints of struggle that my life endured to get me
hear. I saw my mistakes where I thought no hope could
abound and yet I struggled to a hopeless destination
that betrayed my presumptions and the land still
beckoned my calloused feet. My agonies did leave mark
of where I had traveled, where evil did perspire in my
heart humility called me back to a godly trek despite
my endless failures. How much must I fall back to the
cesspool and let God gently forgive and forgives
I cannot say? I must admit for all my failures I am
reminded that it is all mercy that continues to allow
me to dream. My bones ache in sympathy seeking sweet
release yet my heart desires that I spread the gore of my
existence to bring life to this draining grey. I sought

to find value in my life but only through suffering
did I find beauty in this existence. Only through the
diamond tears can light truly shine in this place. Only
through scarlet blood exerted on these plains can
beauty show her exuberant color. Only through the
dusty white bones left across the land can purity know
it's true. Only through the darkest nights can the
stars reveal the vastness of all creation. Only through
the smallest lives that make up the masses can our
insignificance seem so much larger and true. I sought
greatness in the sun-streaked sky and could not find
glory in the burning sun but the millions of distant
suns that grace us with a kinder distance than our
burned bodies are so used to. I could not find any relief
in life's urgings so I sought beauty in suffering that I
might have some worth in the cold world that left no
remorse for a wary soul caught in its heated dribble. My
song is not through voice of an angel's choir nor the
transcending beauty of perfect voices but through the
aching bones, sobbing agony and seeping sobs of a painful
existence. These hardships provide the ink to deliver
my life's song in hope for a better ending in a world of
endless irony and contradictions.

BROKEN TIES

You came to me with broken ties
Confused about people's ways
I took you into heart as a sister
I believed great things that you could proclaim
I saw you like family such a close friend
Our heart talks brought life to my forsaken ways
I thought I could call you and express such pains
and lean a shoulder for when you hurt all the day

I only wanted to be a blessing
I did kind things because big brothers love to
spoil their little sisters besides a tease or two
I never had strong family ties

I was a black sheep that was never understood in my ways
I looked to you to be a sister, but you took
that knife and severed our friendship away
You insulted me and betrayed my trust
and threw me into a rage

Though you had much evil intent in your heart
towards me I tried to love you as my sister
You spoke not to me of what troubled you in your pain
You looked upon me as a monster who

desired to steal your fame

You heard not my cries for just the truth

You destroyed my faith in healing this day

In anger I broke into infernal rage

You stood by and smiled at this display

You proclaimed innocence and declared me an oppressor

Twice not once you sent others to do your bidding

Who understood not what had occurred?

Who came to me as if I was an

oppressor and made me feel evil

Twice you destroyed my trust and thrice it shall not be

I still care to where I would love to see you free,

but until than you are Satan's slave to be

I will forgive and pray of healing to

come to me, but until then this curse I

shall endure till Christ set me free

THE MINDS METAMORPHOSIS

Finally, I have reserved this section for a new period
of my life. I now consider myself non-religious but
still love and appreciate the good I can take out of
Christianity while leaving behind the ceremonial
aspect of religion. My latest works reflect on my
attitude toward an examination of the evils of
mankind and the dangers of using religion to steal
and cheat people out of their money. This collection
of poetry spans over 14 years of writing at different
points of my life and I wanted to show my transition

BRIMSTONE PREACHING

I walked that holy path seeking only lies trying to find purpose in this parody I am living. You ensured my life was full of fear and lead me down a path of servitude and joyful affliction. I trusted you to care and what was not convenient was a joy to forget as I laid there bleeding out my soul. Held down and made to feel the shame I was painted with and told my suffering was justified to share the agony of others without a hand to hold back those who would steal our innocence and leave us to bleed out our soul and slowly die. I am so, fucking goddamn sick of holy people telling me my suffering was justified. I fucking want to die and leave these memories to the void and escape this hell where every thought is evil and I must be reminded to bleed. Fuck your god and your blood gold. Fuck your golden idol you love so much to raise on a pedestal of blood, flesh, and bones. I lay here dying inside and you all you can say is just to give it all to Jesus Christ. No ears to hear the teardrops, no hand to wipe away the sorrow or blood. Just the empty hollow footsteps of holy men coming to fix us because they could not fix themselves and they painted a scarlet letter on us least we are free from shame. Their conviction and condemnation eat away at us but we are holy by the cleansing of holy fire yet all you left were our burnt corpses and broken minds

but we are holy, we are holy, we are holy, we are empty,

hollow and broken but so long as we are hollow you are

happy to preach and watch us bleed.

FOOTSTEPS

I can hear their echo in the distance where I once walked and the echoes of the past remind me of a man long lost to the madness he conceived in agony. I can't identify with myself as I don't recognize the man I was or understand the madness he adopted and I am separate from myself. Never the one for recruitment or endless chanting I fell away from hell's condemnation that I might be delivered to eternal regret in eternal limbo. To fall away into fire because I could not find life within. This figure that stalks me is not me but is. I don't recognize what I lived and the haze that comes with these regrets leave me to wander choking on the fog of this distant reality. This figure I hear him coming closer to close in and try to end my sin filled life. He haunts me because he can find no solace being lost to time and convictions long withered that once held me down. I won't go back to that personal hell where my only promise is death and hellfire and a forever disappointed god. The footsteps fall silent and I can hear no more. What I am beyond this veil and the bridge that lead to that dark cave fell. The stalking was naught but a faint memory of darkness that once plagued my life. What was once full of life did die to faith that could never justify. I can't go back to where ghosts stalk and lie because I have no faith left in me. Tonight, I shall dine alone for the first time and no longer will those footsteps haunt my life. I forgot what I was and only know what I am and the man that was, is gone and lost forever.

SEVERED LIMBS AND PARTS

Who am I or what am I, I cannot tell, my identity is
stripped from me. What I saw in hope with a heart that
cared for the broken and poor and I could identify
with his pain but his followers who took me molded
me into something foreign, something I could not
understand and it filled me with blind rage attacking
all the wrong shadows. I found myself in a foreign
mind that could never meld with what I really was. The
parts of me that are my building blocks rage within me.
I severed their connection and denied their existence.
I never recognized what I saw in reflections as their
countenance did not match what I felt inside. These
parts of me scattered to the desert rotting in the sun
will not forget their ostracization. They tear at me
to get back within but all that's left is an empty void.
Now I look to a new future with a new body. The parts
must be recognized lest I fall back into a pile and rot.
To unite is to become what I am and recognize what was
stolen and live as I was made rather than what others
want.

SONAR IDENTITY

Music is powerful and the kind of music we like often reveals what kind of person we are inside and reflects our thoughts and feelings. Music is our identity, our foundation of who we are. We flow like a river to that which appeals to our heart and we can never force ourselves to like anything other than what speaks to our soul. Our aspirations, dreams, and hopes translate into the sounds we parade with pride. Everyone's tune is the greatest sound when in the midst of their bliss. We are bound by the sounds we hear within and inside.

Don't ever deny what the heart cannot lie. Give in to the sounds that speak and live through their testimony. Live the sound that heals the identity and walk to a tune that burns within and gives life to what is our design and image. Let us live in the moment where music ministers to us what we feel. When you cannot see in the mirror what you behold than using the ears to behold the image in the sounds eye. Great vibrations screeching through the air and my form do begin to appear. I speak through the songs that I hold dear, the words that write me into being lead me from the fog and I followed the tunes and learned who I really am.

GREEN RUSH

Here I sit looking in a haze as the Mary jane moves through me. My mind is open my body is calm as I take in the beauty of nature's gifts to me. Every puff engages me every thought and takes me to another place. The circles of our hearts pleasure bring us all together. Life is so vibrant when I feel a green rush coming into me. The scent, the taste delivers me from myself and is the heaven that God has given. Pure of essence, pure of mind I sit here and deliver my soul from the tyranny of reality. So, little I can hold, so precious is the moment I am filled for evil men seek to destroy peace by promising fool's hell. They flock to their buildings of refuge holding back their tears leaving bitter preaching to the plant that would usurp their claws from our hearts and let us be free. They take in the green rush and hold us back from what would deliver us from the web the rich spun to hold us down. We must unite least our cause does die and take to the streets and demand the hypocrisy ends. The cure to mankind's afflictions are locked within the green rush and instead of healing we are fed poison so we can die. You cannot live, you cannot exist, you must desist and lay down and never resist. I refuse this, I refute your claims of superiority. I stand tall on a pedestal with a loud voice to demand the end to hells tyranny. This is my body; my mind and my soul yet wicked fools seek to hold me captive

and watch me slave away. Rebel, rebel against the fools

and sadists that hold us down. We can't breathe so long

as you hold us down and it's time to make a stand and

demand a death to a system that punishes progress and

will deliver us from the soul's poverty.

DARKNESS IS A PERSPECTIVE

Inspiration I am your Slave. I cannot escape the realities of who I am. The deep self-hatred and sadistic nature to mutilate. What is the sick impulse in me that cannot satisfy until I see the blood running down and polluting my flesh? That vibrant coppery scent that decadent flavor that sends me to ecstasy. I cannot deny the freak in me, the hunger for blood I seek and the taste is ever so fleeting and oh so wrong when we wish to consume. Fuck this lust in me to desire my blood pooling at the end of a knife or the fountains from the right push pin to release this torment in me. This torment inside me eats away my soul and leaves me this husk. Am I obsessed or merely convinced that the blood is bad and must be shed but the unholy consumption is to find some value in this fucked up world that fucked up my mind. Am I wicked according to the account of the factory outputs? I am dark, I am dead inside, I am a plaque, I am the unwholesome impulse in the back of your mind that fucks with your identity before you become a factory output or if you will suffer individuality to tear you up and throw you into the air like confetti. Twisted mentalities, broken realities, mindless wandering, constant agony, leave me in a state of constant revolting. Never sate your appetite with boring consistency, live in revolt against the established mentalities. I am trapped by these images and in a state of constant mobility. On this river of identity, I change from one to another and we are reborn in ideologies and baptized in my fears. You think I am the freak, have you seen how your exact identities are terrifying to me. I cannot rest until I find another freak to display our loving eccentricities. Fuck the system and its predatory sick old men looking for young flesh to sate their lust. Before you judge my eccentricity, I point out your heroes disgusting appetites and sadistic idiosyncrasy and hypocrisy.

THE NEXT EVOLUTION

I can hear the echoes in the distance. A man I never knew who is speechless and dead deep inside. The distant patter of rain on another plain. The distance to this plane is right in front of our face and the distortion of what we believed to be real is shimmering in a pale dissolution to the puddles of our minds these holes in our existence, these deep wells of realities we cannot see. The 4th dimension is just a little out of my sight, I can see it, I can feel it just right. To blur the realities of what are conscious tries to convey to us other truths. We peel back the layers of conventional thought and replace our minds with the reversal of sight. I can hear others in the distance but I cannot quite make out their speech. I feel like the plaque on my mind has melted away and I can once again see beyond dark veils that hid me away. I can see now colors and perception that could not quite unveil itself to me. I am transcendent in my conscious thought and I can see past the numb barriers that held me down. I am just on the outside looking in and what I see is not what I feel. A third option to rather heads or tails but perhaps a new design found on the next dimension we can glimpse from a distance and just make out a greater design of connected hearts and minds that seek to meld. We are trapped in shells only so long as we willingly allow our conscious to be prisoner to our superego. I must slip past the parts of our minds and fill in the blanks so again all should be so well. We commune as one without knowledge or conclusion. We cannot see ourselves until we first deny ourselves our delusions. The more certain a man is, the more uncertain is his foundation. He is trapped to a consciousness that refuses to allow expansion into other realities. To evolve beyond the simple three-dimensional trap, we have existed in but to become something more, something eternal. Deja vu is familiarity for a reason. It is a reminder that we have done this before and we'll do it again. Our energy can never expire but transpire into something greater. We are united in our diversity and strong in our stand against those who would hold us hostage to the world we were told was our foundation when our minds are the gates to something grander.

WEED THE PEOPLE

We the people of the United States, in order to form
a more perfect Union, establish Justice, insure domestic
Tranquility, provide for the common defense, promote
the general Welfare, and secure the blessings of liberty
to ourselves and our posterity, do ordain and establish
this Constitution for the United States of America.
We demand the immediate end to the drug wars and
the DEA and establish our rights as citizens to be free
in our choices and consequences yet allow for the safe
treatment of those who have learned the folly of hard
drugs. Marijuana is not a hard drug and in fact is the
safest and most healthy drug to consume and therefore
it is not only a massive abuse of the U.S. Constitution
but is spitting in the face of freedom and the founding
fathers who took great pleasure in the use of hemp
and marijuana. It is not up for the government to be
our parents and continue to abuse us in a perpetual
war never meant to be won but to suppress the rights
of the people for profit. We as a people demand the
restoration of the Constitutional rights to be a
document protecting the rights of the people as opposed
to being a plaything for the rich and corporations. We
the people demand the government stay out of our lives
so long as we do not hurt other and demand that the

crime of greed be recognized and punished harshly as almost no crime can parallel to the damages created by severe avarice. Such a luxury should not be tolerated in the U.S. and neither should it be rewarded in the world abroad. The unethical and cruel punishment of criminals must be reformed to rehabilitate and not to agitate criminals in the goal of severely reducing our incarceration rate and lowering crime simultaneously.

Capitalism should never have engulfed our justice system and perpetrated mass rape of the people. Weed the people of the United stoners, in order to perform a more perfect high, establish drug rights, insure domestic integrity, provide for the common defense of drug users, promote the general welfare of its citizens as drug use is a health issue, not a criminal issue, and secure the blessings of joint liberty to ourselves and posterity, do ordain and establish in the Constitution the right to blaze in the United States of America. This is our declaration to end the hateful and racist war on drugs and end the violations of civil liberties against minorities and the LGBT community. We stand united against this violation of our rights and liberty and refuse to bow to your imperialistic tyranny.

JUST WONDERING

I was just wondering if you could ever see a situation where you are in the wrong and your pathetic cries are just another platitude to play to ignorance in reaping sympathy. I wonder if you enjoyed the tears or needed another soul to bear your misery and crucify my heart for your sins and just lie here absorbing your pain and seeking resolution in my own existence. I cannot for the life of me understand why you ever wanted me. If I was your problem, you could have cut me out like a tumor instead all I can do is look at you in shock and wonder. Do you recognize my face, do you see the scars you left all over me? So, you suffered from cruel afflictions but it's a little hard to distinguish stories from reality because with you, you never really realized who you were and what you stood for but absorbed in those god damn bottles. I was just a problem to block your indulgences, I was fodder for your rage that you poured in me. I cannot think for myself surely so you planted what you could and I could see the truth from fiction and I suffered so you could find some comfort in your self-inflicted misery. I don't mean to discount your crocodile tears but those tears burned into my soul and I never really understood the agony you left in me. How many years can you drown in spirits and wrath filled hell before you just admit your hypocrisy and account for all your cruelty. I am curious how you will react to the truth when you see it. Will it blind you and to your knees will you fall and the agony shall overtake and will you repent or fill up mercy with more lies to comfort the sin you placate to. Tell me how you expect me to feel sorry when you never bothered to care what tore me up. How will you account for so much lost memory, are you even here? Do you register your surroundings anymore or is everything a goddamn dystopia and you are the center of unjust misery? Why did you bother seeking love when you were empty of it from the beginning? Your alcoholic kisses just make me vomit and remember what I lost. I cry but you cannot hear your child's tears over your own. So, I was wondering will you repent or not but I can't help but wonder if it's just too late and you are lost to your imagination and never able to peel back the layers and accept who you are. You are so filled with hate but you cannot understand that it's your accusing reflection that drives you mad. I know because I bleed to keep him back. To take away my shame and take me somewhere far from the reality of this duality. I need to bleed out your poison and deliver myself from the filth and be free but I am trapped in this paradox of life and death. Held in one hand a razor and the other are empty and I need to just know why I should bother. I was wondering when you cared to seek me out but to be honest your absence is heaven to me. Don't expect me to feel sorry for you or give a damn about your paranoid delusions. I was just wondering...then I realized there is nothing left to pity all is dead. I would have worn black but I did not realize I was at a funeral for the living dead seeking to eat and consume. Will you ever get your fill of endless misery or will we have to continue this bull shit merry go round where all I want to do is get off before I puke up my soul and become the husk you are or to find some kind of reason I bother caring anymore.

CIRCLES IN THE SKY

I see them circling above a never-ending torrent of hell's teeth coming from above. The dripping beaks seeking to tear and rend as I lay here broken and nearly dead. Enslaved by the sun's scorching rays that lay upon me. Imprisoned by the desert around me sucking the life from me. The vicious birds demand I starve, they seek out my death and love my thirst. No shelter to hide from the descending circle that seeks my end. Their violent desires a nightmare of the deserts cruel games. No plan, no knowledge no stepping stones to avoid their descent, all is spent in their claws to rend. No aid to mend my wounds but bear the gaze of vultures above. No excuses but their hunger, never mind the dead the flesh tastes of wonder. All my human needs exhausted and stripped from me as vulture's circle down one by one. One is named debt, the other ignorance and of course, hunger. Down from above comes slavery and control lest I break my binds and be free. Violence descends in a great hurry. Homelessness lunges above and imprisonment dive to sate their hunger and above all the one that looms above them all is avarice who motivates them all. Who will come to our rescue, who will seek to free us from the hell of all the others? Who will deny the reasons of deadly men who feast

on blood and flesh of prey they forced down. Little
to know that these vultures who violence has always
known claim to be loving creatures with blood dripping
from their beaks. Give up the fight and forget how you
cling to life for the sky is full of golden birds who
devour great wealth and no one can survive and they
shall surely slowly starve and die. The glutton does not
know his end but these birds shall be the earth's eternal
end. In this age of strife, the poor seek to deliver us
from the rich's earthly delight. Who knows the end
to this story, who knows rather we shall be delivered
or devoured. All I know is there is no reason to feast
forever, take in moderation and you just might live
forever.

BLANK CANVAS

I often wonder where my words shall lead, where my
mind and heart shall lead. Never knowing the words
that will be birthed and know the battle of creativity.
My muses silent often that they may test my resolve
and learn to create on the moment rather art sings or
not at all. I see the blistering white and wonder what
inscriptions I can lay out and dream of other worlds
and place my heart above reality and all. Rather to
hear my cry, rejoice or simple musings is all determined
by what I shall create to show all. I often wonder when
my time will come to unveil my art and reveal my soul
to all. Blood and tears mingled in a pink color is the
greatest ink to unveil my often-darkened heart. Rather
tears of joy or unending sorrow is the revelation one
can tell all. Blood is the life and the inspiration for
all. Shed in agony or the brilliance of life is its toll. I
cannot say what will drive me to pen these thoughts
or what shall be birthed but I let it appear. Blank
canvas can only remain so pure in a world distraught
with empty words. We must write, speak and sing to
unveil what our hearts reveal and we must take to the
stars to know our unlimited potential to create great
worlds beyond. Though the stars lay beyond our reach,
eternal distance yet inspiration they do create. Among

the blackness of space, they do proclaim we exist by our

light and this message of creation continues to resist,

the impulse of a blank canvas that tears us from within.

WHAT TIME IS IT

You walked down a spiral and saw past the clocks that shadowed your every thought. Time is an abstract and what we are now is what we never were and always have been. I sought to placate the rumbling of the giant's hunger but I could not find the pellets of resolution to awake him. This room I am, I recognize it but cannot for the life of me understand where I am. There is no universe unless we will for it to be. Without faith, nothing can exist. I took a glimpse at the destruction to see if I could undo these patterns that blanket the room. Help! I am drowning in this pool of jelly. I don't want to move away, it's so comforting but when I sink can I breathe? The voices that told me I could wake up have gone to slumber and I cannot fathom where their thoughts have gone. I am alone here and I cannot see past this veil. It is so thick and so tattered so as the light comes in as broken shards. Is this vision? The shattered visage of light dimly cast through the curtains. Is not this the pool of all religion and faith whereas the light comes and goes. Are we eternal in any other aspect that our matter can never be destroyed but only transformed. Therefore, the plants that reassure me before I consume them that their purpose is to fulfill a destiny just as I return my meat back to the plants. Are we not a giant circle that envelopes all existence? Are we not one but only in a state

of transference. Is consciousness life or does the earth

boost of true immortality. The earth speaks to me, she

is broken hearted because no one can see her cry in the

night. The wolves of chaos come to seek her out and take

her to the den of their perversions and defile our lands.

We stand united in the division of mankind's arrogance

to dominate whereas our hubris is the seat of our demise.

The moon cries out to us asking when it's safe to come

back as she can only stand as a perplexed spectator. Yes,

even the moon is cheese when truth cannot prove itself

unless we taste of it. I tried a pie and it tasted like earth, I

tried the earth and I tasted the flesh of the savory fruit.

Come ye all seeking answers and look within yourselves

to be born into the revelation of your own creation.

One man's definition is not the road all tread but many

mouths defy truth in declaration of infinite paths. All

signs and guidelines of various degrees leading us to

destinations we cannot unveil until we transcend this

twisted, distorted concept of reality. The mad hatter is

out and seeking a sail of lunacy to give us some kind of

clarity in this faux reality. We cannot play by rules we

never heard nor understood to exist. Books are lies even

to the author, their message always morphed by the reader

to bear the image he wishes to convey. Can you see the

curves of existence carving into the foundation leaving

notes of history yet the art is never the same yet always

the product infinite variations? All emotions are chaos

and create and destroy the worlds we perceive before us.

To shatter your shades of your perception of existence

than your third eye can finally see the riddle who was

answered but we never knew the words to understand

the question. We are in infancy trying to scramble up the

slopes of perceived destinations yet we wonder forever,

forever we shamble about zombies seeking flesh to sustain.

We adjourn this meeting and declare our proclamation of

the undead conversion least the living absolves us what

we sold. These muses, these oracles look down on us and

dictate our every move and we are but chess pieces to our

creators call and subjection to the muse's rule.

CHAUFFEUR

Life is hard enough with all the choices, let me make things easy and make them for you. Driving through the night let the voices drive you. Close your eyes and let the voices guide you. Hate and pain, a gilded childhood with thorns and brambles. Strength substituted for humanity too numb to drive so I just close my eyes let go of the wheel and let the voices guide me. Awakened from moment to moment in an instance to blink in and out of consciousness. Suddenly I find myself in the middle of TX. Why I am in this desert I don't know I was not driving. While paradise is now behind me, slipped away. I gradually found myself put together. I somehow wound up in New Mexico. Better yet but I am still not certain who is driving.

I gave control to all the different voices and now I don't know where to go so I let the voice that spoke to me, in the beginning, raise me. No mother or father but the angry figures that stood before me. I wake up from my consciousness and I see myself pissing on plants to grow them. All this time I wondered why everything I ate tasted like piss and shit. I would care had someone not been using my food as a toilet. It's kind of hard to not shit where I eat when rich fools enjoy stooping so low. I would not have been feasting on trees had I ever known there was a difference. By the way who the fuck

is driving?

THE NEW GOD

Mine gold is mine leader, I shall want more. Cupiditas makes me enslave small children, Cupiditas leads me besides fields of oil.

Cupiditas fills me with avarice, he leadeth me in the path of wickedness for my own gain.

Yea though I walk through the valley of paupers, I shall fear no poverty, mine riches are with me, mine avarice and apathy watch over me.

Cupiditas prepares slaves for me in the presence of my competitors, thou anointest my head with gold, my riches know no end

Surely avarice and apathy shall follow me all the days of my wealth and I will dwell in the houses of others for the rest of my days.

VIOLATED PUPPET

Who takes to let us dance around and find ourselves
deep in another town where the mind does bend and
the soul does rend to the sound of those god forsake
bells. Another pill, another swallow to make the gloom
brighten all around but I can see in the reflection
of the TV my audience through a black veil. I see you
watching me, I see you pulling the strings, I see you
taking advantage of me. I would scream rape but no
one could see the hands partake and violate. Why must
you take away our rights and shove your hands deep
inside? Why must you move my mouth through pictures
of imagined hell where my soul goes to die? Where am
I in this theater because I am all too often not sure
if I am in a comedy or tragedy and often it seems like
life is a smash of countless realities. So here I mope and
like the willow pulsating in the moon's glow my tears
slowly inch to the pool of my endless woe. How often
have I come to these crossroads, how often have I come
to these paths of divisive converse? How often do I
find myself split between blinding light and comforting
darkness, addicted to the confines of this pit...but I
found when I stare into the light long enough all
becomes dark and I eventually I can no longer see the
light so really what is the difference but a perspective

in time? Rather you linger in the blinding light or into the darkened night we are all still puppets robbed of our sight. Within this light, I see the lines and hooks embedded in flesh, oh God help me I cannot pass this test all life is just one big fucking mess. I feel the hand moving my body and my head, the pain of manipulation is all the violation. God help me, I'm a fucking puppet just waiting to die but the words they speak through my mouth filled with endless hate betray the gloomy soul seeking to find solace within my days. I cannot speak for all are lies when the puppet master comes to take away what little pride. I can only scream deep within, deep inside...

WHO'S LAUGHING NOW

Come all, come all, come to see what boasts of great
hilarity. This great display of drama in human history.
Rather color or nationality or simple religiosity
we were all divided and categorized as enemies. We
hold true to the fact we must wear the star-spangled
blindfold of our loving patriotic march into the
factories that turn us into a cannibal lunch. We are
a spectacle to fight amongst us all when the enemy is
the ones who stand tall. We bear our hearts to fight
this fight and take the land from those without sight.
When your heart burns with hate for another who
is just another victim to similar fates you must learn
who laughs at your prodigy. Trapped in a cage, limitless
potential, we all can take up to the mantle. We sit and
we wait in these cages, rats trapped in a corporate lab.
Our cheese is our poison that we seek and we forget
we can chew through the walls and fucking escape.
There is no winning in this war so long as we subject
ourselves to frivolous waste. All is flesh and weak and
no heart can beat to a perfect leap but we all fall short
and we all fall down, why not pick each other up and
charge. Racism was invented in the rich man's lab to
take what little we all have. How can you claim to be
a master race when you don't even know who to really

hate? It is not by birth by which we must be judged but by our actions and no other. The tragedy of the human condition belongs not only for the rich but all our hearts own to this grief. Only in their loss of humanity is the true tragedy we must understand least we cease to exist. Take up our call, take up our fight, for tonight we dine in hell as we decline. Laugh all you want, chop it up to fidgety conspiracies but when your number is up and they come for your tiny cup you will have to ask who is laughing now for certain it is

not us.

PEELING AWAY THE SHADES

I can't stop scratching the surface of my flesh, peels of human remain falling as flaky raindrops to the floor like shed hair. I sought to find behind the layers some kind of sight beyond this existence that cannot be real. The more I peel back and seek the blood the more my thirst is sated to see the fluids of my pain leaving in a hurry down the drain. I sit here contemplating where I have been and have I ever been in true conviction or did I create this alternate reality to give justice to engravings in my flesh that peel away. They captured me, held me in darkness and blinded me with their light. My flesh was burned and cleansed by fire but all I see is the flaky remains of what I was being replaced by burning flesh eternally ensnared in your guilt laden pleas to stay within a circle drawn by clowns in disguise seeking to hold us to their false ideals in hydrogen blimps of hot air only a pinprick from hellish demise. Such is the house of cards that trembles in the subtlest gusts. We seek some kind of resolution from the world we perceive but when we are blinded by the light of the world we must seek our inner sight from what we feel around. All is connected in its individuality. Free from prying eyes of travesty we fail to look within to find the puzzle pieces we seek to put together from within. So much easier with a guidebook but such myopic perceptions of reality

fail to stand to test our resolve in seeking the good

in society in our own way. Woe to the man who fails

to fulfill himself in his purpose for it is by our purpose

we find a purpose to exist. None can escape the web of

deception that entangles the mad and broken. I scream

but you cannot hear, I bang on the walls and proud

with my might until I fall exhausted and wake in a

stupor on the floor without such an utter. The echoes

of the screams that reside within me scratch and claw

at the fabrics that bind them to release their agony in

vengeance to a world that did deny their rotten flesh.

The meat they pick from their teeth to cast at us is self-

evidence in their cannibalistic tendencies. Don't tell

me I am here when my consciousness bleeds into realities

you cannot yet perceive. I don't belong in this world

any more than the water that swirls into the drain.

I am cast from the porcelain hell to descend into the

threads of this pretentious reality. I am slipping into

the abyss of what I cannot ever know. Take yourselves

from the confines of man-made instruction booklets

on how to mutilate their commands into our flesh. We

burn with the greatest sins while denouncing ourselves

to the crowds that come to watch and gawk at the

madness within. Escape while you can before you get
stuck in a cycle of whispers to empty air. I am dying and
the vultures can only find a smirk at the price tag of my
earthly confines. I am already dead and just awaiting
the fucking eulogy.

THIS ALL SEEMS TO FAMILIAR

I am bitter in my grave and my roots that sink deep into thee. I wrap around your soul and seep into you to judge your essence absorbed into me. I am that which birthed you to the world, rather you shine your light or embrace darkness is not your apparel but how you treat the world. No religious ordinance can free the guilty from their sins. Rather we should weight our sins upon our backs that we may not turn back to wicked ways. Let our guilt be the bile that repulses us from old sins. I am lost to the world, untouched and repulsed of every soul. A heart that surely shall only beat alone.

I have watched the world age with hardly a wary thought of chaining myself to be slave and nothing at all. I value my freedom and frown upon the institution of bondage which just results in bitter divorce. No point in mingling lives that will only tear away the safe walls. If I sound bitter, it is because I am. I make no illusion about the wrath of existence on this plane. This anger and rage that feeds me from deep within. I was kept alive by guilt that sought my death. Punishment for escape, eternal hells within, cannot escape the accident of my existence. I would go back if I could and clasp the cord of life till death takes ahold of me and I could drift into freedom within. Alas, I must be punished so I must breathe. Every breath hurts from memories that torment me deep within. The haunting melody of endless regrets and promises hold me at bay in this pit deep inside. You say there is a god-shaped hole in everyone yet the emptiest souls I have borne witness to were the holy bearers of god's light. Golden glows from endless free treasure from the paupers and plebeians we can loot and leave to rot in their graves. You twisted your promise to me by breaking my bones to match your frame, draining my blood to feed me your toxic existence, flaying my flesh and stapling a white lamb's skin to my broken frame. My broken legs, my pride, my identity leave me trapped in this condemning hell. Promises of freedom from guilt but only poison to those who are not absolved of unearned guilt. Such dark desires where we go to be punished as we were raised as kids. We seek that same condemnation to justify the flows of blood flowing over our sundered skin. The horrors of religion testify before the false spirituality in hate-filled primitive thoughts of us against them. Without religion, we are free to pursue spirituality in a way that blossoms into our beauty and not another's idea of spirituality. There is no guide for the soul and spirit only a loose grasp on our own realities. We are but a pebble in the sand. Infinite existences with chaotic patterns. I found more spirituality in the secular sounds of a hopeful heart than in the choirs singing such sweet lullabies to lull the sheep asleep. I crave the edge of existence and pull some reassurance of relief from this earthly shell but only the final dead know their plight or rest. Can our spirits, our sentience transcends the earthly form into a higher form or simply be recycled back into the universe. I cannot tell but I lay at the threshold of my agony seeking an end and my curiosity begs to push forward and see the end. The temptation is gnawing as the end of the world is dawning but I still stand bearing witness to the horror of this world. I must see to its end to satisfy some grand scheme by hands unseen. I know not what puppet show we are to what ends but I know none the fewer strings often wrap around our necks and snap. This distortion of our reality wakes us to the knowledge of our death. Waking up is that choice to move on and only when we seek to divulge our life will our eyes shut eternal and the secrets shall divulge into the twinkling of our light.

YOUR ATTENTION PLEASE

I would speak to you a moment, I would have your ear for a second if you would open your eyes for a moment to see the blood trail you left behind but excuse me sir you killed dignity and left me to die. No guilt, no shame or remorse for these godless games but excuses for why I cry and slowly die inside. I hid in the hole in my heart you dug and sewed it shut. You may have seen it spewing pus and vile juices but never mind that is just my dead child. Me myself and I cannot exist when in youth I did die. Excuse me sir you left a little blood on your shoes, perhaps when you stepped on me to tie me a noose. I can't feel my legs where you broke them with conventional wisdom. How can I walk your path when all sinners must bare their flesh for the searing, burning images to justify torture endless? From youth on up told to embrace it but can you tell me sir how the dead can live when you already drained us. I guess I should succumb to the darkness and lie down to expose this but what good is it to bleed and cry when there is no hope for life. Go about your way, go and rape the world awaiting because after all life is all just over rated.

TWO FACED

This crystal before me does screech, the hollow terror of its face does only match in the numb embrace. These dualities of our separate realities. Two fears faced at two different times. These hearts and minds don't match yet they share the same body. I am alone here in this place where convictions thwarted by higher logic. My anger only matched by my resolve to never again fall to eternal temptations. How can this be to transform my soul and mind? Nothing matters but that I find myself in these translucent thoughts. Tell me clock of your existence. Time is your leash to this plane but across the stars time holds no sway. How can I exist in the same place with vastly different energies? I exist in millions of moments that has no measure but by the standards the sun has given to me.

REDNECK PARADISE

Sitting around without a thought or clue, glued to
the screen and what I I simply cannot believe this simply
cannot be but I do believe we live in a red neck paradise
oh god damn the fucking humanity. The howls and
broken record telling me the same damn lyrics I heard
all these days to this point. The commanding spirit that
excited this nation lying in a golden gutter gurgling
and coughing up the blood from capitalist injections.
Laying hear with a gun to my head unsure if I want
continue watching this tragedy. Children playing with
their nukes with slick sweaty finger hovering above like
some impending dark clouds. The world is in a tailspin
and I am drunk on expectations to the end of this god
damn tragedy. I don't want to be some hero taking the
fall to open closed eyes and I am still sitting here and
seeing the clouds even as I take this dank drag and blow
out my world all these pests swarming all around and
biting at my feet, I trip, I fall and shatter and it's all
just gone. When will I wake up from this dream and live
in a world not starved, a world where personal choice is
not a crime and people no longer horde. Still I cannot
believe here we sit on the edge of a knife slowly dividing
us in a slow agonizing divide. I know the hearts of the
many fall as petals denied of their brilliance and forced
to live a lie.

TIMES TRANSITION INTO LIFE

When the time comes upon us and our existence demands payment where we shall meet again beyond the sight of our mortal wounds. To haul our dreams and stories onward to expand on humanity. Where the sand melts into infinite our minds may once again touch and the requiem of our rest be renewed in new stories to tell. Rest young soul, your incubation will carry on into worlds beyond our fold and we shall glide into the distance over fire paved seas into our next reality and remember the transition to our next journey is the promise of glorious eternity.

TWISTED FANGS

This twisted story that is life weeps from my heart and divides within me the compassion I yearn for yet cruelty is laid on my palms and the nails are driven in to hold me down. The twin scarlet fangs that wind down my legs bear the river of tears and blood where conjoined these pink tears shed from my life is the ink in which my quill draws from the bowl of translucent display of agony. I threw the paint of filth that was spoon fed to me as I rose from the grime. The only cleansing from the vile swamp my body was left to absorb were the hot tears that paved paths down my broken form. My shriveled form lay basking in the shadowed rays of a desert hell. I am consumed by withering agony that is the parasites consuming me. I walk alone on this path for want of just one other. To hold and melt into to draw back into warm covers. For the sake of staying awake these needles I jam into my fingers to test the threshold of my numb flesh deadened by years of cold denial. The cold is bitter and I cannot feel beyond these damn needles that allow me to bleed. Watch for my mural on these frosty walls where the pink tears are frozen on with a story that is often told with a million variations as the sullen snow.

A LAND TO CALL OUR OWN

There is a place my friend among the stars lit upon heavens foundation. Our hearts may lead to a better land where dreams are reality and we can find our place and hope is abundant in these open fields. To run among the spirits of the wild and know mother nature once again. Hold these dreams as close as one can, least the torrents of sorrow seek to wash you away. Hold tight to the natural beauty of heavens touch and seek the colors of universal acceptance. The clouds are our promise that the sky is open to our endeavors. There is no end to where we shall wonder and embrace a much kinder future. No monsters to hold us back in our minds eye where we shall finally find peace.

DEMOLISHING SAND CASTLES

Quickly take turn to hold the candle, reveal through the dark fog. We have held within our hands the brilliant light that binds our heart within. We hold these truths to be self-evident in economic equality we shall all seek. Value has low appeal for services of the human soul least you ride on top the waves of arrogance. Those whose soul is sold to gold reside within the sewers of inequality. The voices rise as a chorus demanding their lives have worth. Society is poisoned with apathetic trolls lacking human hearts. We will rise as the tide and sweep clean these infernal sand castles. Their wealth ill gained will spread to the winds and the people robbed will hold the heads as trophies and the scarlet trails will lead us to the vice that bears these infernal souls. Their worth weighed and found wanting. Slay ambition that burns away our souls and seek deeper treasures that hold us strong. Take comfort in history who holds us accountable for yet another revolution against the greedy parasites of gold.

THE FATE OF ICARUS

Take your wings off and plummet to the place where the
broken and destitute congregate lime a scarlet river
of human misery. Come visit us in this place and peel
the flesh from your eyes and see us for what we bear on
our flesh trees. See the tears flowing into the river,
a toxic hell of human suffering is the river Styx you
commanded we cross to be free of our sight in heavens
high homes where the hearts of hell cannot be in the
pit designed for us yet their souls are worthy of where
our bones lay bare and we hold the knife to sign the
lease on our worthless lives yet the blessed shall know
eternal rage once we stir from our eternal slumber.
Should you not come to see what dark hearts have
wrought we shall drag you to our world and you shall
contribute your dark blood. Our cry shall become you're
the marker of your tomb and no one shall mourn the
broken remains of destitute families the people suffered.
Shed your wings or die in our hell and be condemned
for your perfect life at the expense of our backs and
labor. We are stirred and in time we shall rise and rip
away your holiness and bear the dark sins you tainted
our souls await.

GAZE OF ETERNITY

I stare into space lost in thought, twisted in sight. The fabric of my being is lost to the infinite resolutions that falter and fail. The egg of creation is but thinly cracked and the knowledge we possess is not even a pebble on infinite sands. Discovery with no end and yet vast knowledge hides the key of revelation. Among the swirls of memory, we our lost in the history of mankind where the experience of all envelopes me in the sea of eternal uncertainties. Madness...I touch the fringe of the tattered curtains of creations well. I drink deeply and lose touch of false realities and eternally I slumber in the confines of my myopic mind. Rest...so far yet so near into the eternal requiem of my confinement indeed. Hear my scream and learn my agony of the trap of eternal ignorance. A darkness that looms yet I shall forever chase the setting sun never losing sight of new discoveries.

THE LAST KISS

What is this mistress in which my heart does weep for her comfort yet she does frighten me deep. Such peaceful airs that stir within me to sleep aside her gentle form away from the cares of a dying world. My die is cast and my eyes split with desire and dread to hold my mistress eternally I cannot choose and fate waits so lazily. I cling to freedom as her desire grasps my heart unsure of where rest lies, unsure of where my soul does reside. I hear her calling on the wind her shadowed form whispering to me from the void I seek with dread. The spidery tangles that weave their thread do engulf me warm comfort from scarlet threads winding their way around my limbs envelope me to spread me over gentle air. I am uncertain if I reside with her or if it's all a hazy dream. I long for her touch, her silent song a blissful memory of the abyss. The love of her is forbidden though I know not why when she comforts me in solace where no longer shall I have to cry. I love her with all my spirit and cling with desire to which I cry to the heavens why must it be forbidden if this love is written in our fate why not let us go on with the date to embrace her sweet invitation to live splendid. Peace, rest and all above fairness. This is heaven is it not where my mistress has her place for those who are wicked

and those who are not. We can all embrace under the
shadow of my lovers embrace where all is equal and fair.
A land where there is no hate, no greed, no apathy. A
land that is just for all and we no longer have to cry
and bleed. Why should we not welcome such love openly.
Fear not but embrace her call mankind it is our saving
grace from our eternal fall. Come one, come all to
embrace our goddess who embraces us all. My mistress,
my love come at once least we expire and our souls be
lost. My love come to me through the blissful glade
of heavens symphony and let us forsake man's foolish
wisdom. Our love cannot be denied and the world is
worthy of this lust. Let us partake of forbidden love
and embrace the shadows that loom high above and
drink in the end of plight giving us eternal new sight.
Yes, my mistress I call you to heed that you shall hold
me deep indeed. The ultimate embrace from the sweet
tender kiss of my mistress and all shall be right indeed.

BAPTIZED IN FIRE

The entangling spider webs of translucent memories spinning deep within me. The buzzing swarms of angry thoughts drown me out and leave me in stuttering shambles. My mind took a hold of me and puppeteer my every action and word. A cadaver soaking in the sun, a bleak gaze lost in fog. The fiery waves drown him in a dark haze. The notes of sunlight searing as musical notes. The moon reflected on a rivers edge leads to her twin caught in the reflection two worlds merge forge the universes into a mold of our blind perspectives into eternity. My numb thoughts leave my body numb to the raging pain within. As parasites emerging from the cavity within my body spikes the agony of the river of distant memories. Those screaming howls of rage enveloping me. Concealed within this infernal shell baked by all this fucking hate. I am birthed from a darkness no soul can adorn. Light abandons me in this godless fate. Never can I trust the shades that often visit me. Do I revel in this thirst for relief from this mortal shell? Do I stand and proclaim, my voice shattering the air as glass stabbing the earth with such force? Come with me into the asylum of my mind and partake of the madness that burns from within.

LOST DREAMS

Oh, woe is me whom love did grievously deny me. To feel that ilk, that sickness of the soul when the heart seeks his other side. Her gentle voice, her loving eyes, who did put a spark in my life. My uttered words I will regret until I die, the secrete of my hated desire to be by her side. This was invoked with a bitter laugh and cruel denial. Rather I have never known than to incur her bitter mockery. What was precious to my very soul drove her away from me where friendship died because of that sickening desire. Whom am I but Apollo seeking the hand of Daphne who despised his love and was driven from he, her form forever transformed into a tree. As such this tree is my bitter roots in longing for what would never be. Her memory a long-tortured thought is all I may do, in honor of honest love made true. Such a pleasure it would be that I could treasure your heart without your knowledge that our time might have been forever indeed. When you wondered far from me, I wished for your company again to kindle in blissful friendship but nay my heart could not hold out and buckled from living a lie. My vow of death to the heart that betrayed, I swore an oath to kill the desire of my other and with blood did I make this unholy pact and brought death to my soul, forever consumed indeed.

RESTING PLACE

I must aspire to the fields of green where my heart came
to grieve. The jotted landscape where memories held
free do create the storm within me. I hold a candle
in these cold winds where bones creek old. Where the
whispers of ancient echoes consume my every thought.
The spirits do wave in the wind, such sweet melodies
adrift in the air. My mortality a looming expression, a
wretched grin. The sight of life's thin strain, stretched
to the brim. My sullen cries dying on short breaths
within.

WORD PAINT

Words are but paint in which we begat upon this world
our spirit and light. Upon the pool of creativity, we
reflect unto the world our sight. In our madness we
delve deep into creativity. For that which we can bear
no sight the mad dip into insanity. For only can we see
beyond the veil of reality and create that which never
existed, a new birth in our world. Only a madman can
behold the world to see its potential. Only with the
touch of insanity can we see beyond the veil. Only we
can perceive alternate realities. We share the power of
gods deep within our hearts. His presence guides our
touch.

HIGH TRAVELS

Flying across the world over fire paved blazing seas, chasing the sun to gain back what darkness took from me. Above the heavens, a kingdom of clouds the sky presents to me. Not quite keeping up with the suns pace the day succumbs to night, flying across many lands and the great sea. I delve into the motion of force that holds me high and soar the stars feeling sweet victory. A trillion lights merging on the horizon, I sought wisdom from their grateful touch. Immortal light ages old yet always fresh to the glee of our sight. Burning away the fuel till I finally find my destiny and stop chasing the sun infinitely.

A WELL LIVED LIFE

This poem was dedicated to my uncle who always could
bring family together and made the best food
From early on destiny held you tight to write the story
of Bennie's full life. A tale of a young man who found
strength among the seas. Tossed from wave to wave
yet none could sink his resolve to fight through the
cold depths of Poseidon's infamy. The spirits of history
watched over your march and lifted you among the
ancestor's flight. The ancient line that bore this man
on high shall join him in heavens holy light. We stand
united grieved but firm in delight from the memories
of a man who never bowed before any plight. The wife
he stood by strong in their union was the apple of his
eye. A love story to be told with heavenly delight.
Children strong from his wisdom and insight hold up
his memory to uplift their own lives. Hear lies a man
that our hearts grieve but souls rejoice at all our
wonderful times. Hear lies an American hero who lived
a blessed life. Here lies our friend, eternally with never
forgotten times.

VOICE OF THE SILENT MAJORITY

Sleepless nights where cold and terror grip the heart with fright. Gold paved roads for icy souls who burn for wealth undivided. Untouched wealth massed in banks that never see light while bellies growl with creaky bones screech throughout the night. Work our only mode while greed leaves us forever broke. Echoed words from long ago, condemning the greed that broke the world. A wage to pay, to live with hope, long forgotten by those who never knew. With a thundering voice the thieves were scattered, until the robbers joined to overthrow. Masses whose only desire was to once again see the fire. The beacon to find where our sweet and tears could break our molds. To know a life without debts slavery most of us have known. A broken system where only wealth leads the world. Pure hearts weary of systematic abuse, until a voice once again begin to rise. The choir of the broken and poor, demanding retribution from unrelenting masters. A thunder arises for the masses. A hope to end what greed began. A leader whose hands bear clean and lived with consistency. A champion of the people who demanded a return, to when our labor had merit and slavery only a bad memory. Bernie stands with us, a true American hero.

THE MESSAGE

Those words echo deep reverberating, crushing my essence, boiling my soul, poured into an empty vessel and drank deeply of what was old. The thoughts that plagued me, the words that ate at me pierced the shroud and revealed unto me the division of the heart, mind and soul. This triangular immortality uplifts us to defy death and be marked eternal by our scars, battles and tears that hold us down. The fire of knowledge burns hot and seers our blackened souls. We delve into the abyss of time where measurements defy reality and how can we age and die when the universe does deny our arrogant display of pride to limit time to the constraints of our will. Rather as opposed to liberating us from our own self-inflicted mortality. Outside our planet time warps reality into another dimension of infinity. We cannot even grasp the straws of endless space much less think of all of existence having no boundaries. Surely, we shall never know anything about infinity or immortality. Our existence is a mystery that we shall never uncover. The infinite variations are but separated by endless distance but all the same we are not even microscopic frames within the 4th dimension.

Bonus 2nd edition material. The Minds Cataclysm

Since initially publishing my book, I have changed a lot in the last 3 years and have collected more various poems and narration on what I have come to believe and stand for as a Libertarian Socialist or anarchist. A pacifist who despises violence and destruction but I will always rebel against the stand quo. A joined The Satanic Temple and am now an ordained minister of The Church of the Flying Spaghetti Monster. Atheist religions that reflect on secular reasoning. I am not an official representative of The Satanic Temple but we basically wish ultimate freedom for people as well as respecting the diverse religious beliefs. We don't hate religion; we simply don't want one religion forced on everyone else. We strive to live our lives with honor and goodness and to make up for any evil we did. We just kind of like dark satanic art and the spirit of rebellion. Many of us suffer Religious Trauma Syndrome from having religion forced down our throats and it is a form of empowerment over old toxic beliefs rather it be from persecution to sexuality, race or gender we want the individual to realize the power is within themselves and not from an outside source. The Church of the Flying Spaghetti Monster advocates for teaching of evolution in schools and who is to say God is not a giant flying spaghetti monster.

The point being is I have found doctrines that reflect more about what I believe in as well as embracing the rebel that is in us all to live free so long as we don't hurt anyone. I don't worship the devil of course as I don't believe in his existence but I believe in the spirit of rebellion. An Oscar Wilde quote states,

> "Disobedience, in the eyes of anyone who has read history, is man's original virtue. It is through disobedience that progress has been made, through disobedience and through rebellion." – Oscar Wilde The Soul of Man Under Socialism

Arbitrary rules designed to inhibit individual personal freedom is a tyranny that should no longer be tolerated in our society that is draining us of our creative powers to curb toward worship of basically whoever is preaching. If we are to evolve as humans, we must stop accept absolutes and learn from life as we go or else, we stagnate and cease to grow. When we think we have found the answer another presents itself and the more answers we get the more questions we get. So, I found that doing what we want so long as we hurt no one and have the right to be offensive as well because without offense there is no growth or challenge and getting offended hurts no one. I first will lay out a short book within a book if you want to call it that on my ideas of how we can improve this country and world.

Religious Trauma Syndrome

There is a new diagnosis that should be recognized A new form of CPTSD that is more specific from abuse by controlling religious figures through the use of fear, indoctrination and threats of eternal conscious torture and death if we don't obey. It is known as RTS (Religious Trauma Syndrome) and it's caused by extreme religion and control of people's lives.

Death threats are not free speech. Its violence and it does cause severe psychological and emotional trauma. People in the LGBQT community are especially easy targets for these predators who often cause these people to end their lives, self-harm or cause extreme antisocial behaviors in public such as homophobic marches and protests targeting the LGBQT community because they, themselves are gay. I was once even threatened in a Walmart parking lot and I did not say one word to him because of a Satanist hoodie I wore. I am an Atheist and The Satanic Temple is not about worshiping the devil at all but quite the contrary. It is about self-empowerment, self-acceptance and a right to our own body.

From my experience in the church there is this sado-masochist relationships where the sadists feed on the torment of the masochists and the masochists depends on fulfilling a need of punishment because of mostly illogical guilt. I am not saying everyone is in this kind of relationship though. I am saying the extremists in churches develop these unhealthy codependent relationships. Often the Sadists presents themselves as always right and righteous and will verbally and emotionally attack other members of their organization feeding their need to dominate. The people plagued with toxic guilt feed into that pain to try and alleviate irrational guilt such as sexual feelings for members of the same sex, premarital sex, the music they listen to, the clothes they wear, the food they eat, etc. The masochists often suffer from an inability to see their own power and strength and instead depend on the abuser to guide them no matter how much pain they inflict on themselves.

That is why as a Satanist in The Satanic Temple I am about self-empowerment and finding strength within myself and not a deity I cannot prove its existence. I am my own god and my own master. I am responsible for my actions to those around me, the environment, any living creature and property. Now I need to clarify I am a member of TST but not an official representative so anything I say is of my own opinion and interpretation of the guidelines of TST. For more information about our organization and any questions please visit https://thesatanictemple.com/pages/about-us

America has a severe problem with religious extremism ever since Dwight Eisenhower plastered Christianity all over the country in the 50's. We must remove all references to one specific religion from the public sphere because it is imposing one's beliefs over everyone else's. I am a religious pluralist. Although atheists in regards to faith, I am religious in regards to my personal convictions of how I conduct myself in life. To push your faith as a fact is to do a harm to society in expecting us to form our laws in adherence to what I personally consider mostly cult members.

RTS is a form of Stockholm Syndrome where the victim is compelled to repeatedly go back to their abuser under threats of abandonment, eternal punishment, social exclusion, etc. These methods of abuse perpetuate continued abuse with compliance making the person unable to report being a victim of psychological, emotional and often sexual abuse due to feeling allegiance to the cult. Its difficult to leave an abusive relationship when you cannot see the harm it is doing to you as others can see from the outside.

I have struggled with suicide since I was about 7 years old and had an obsession with death, punishment and suffering. In my youth my masochism started with verbal self-harm, sometimes hitting myself or banging my head on something until it hurt, in my 20s due to an extremist religion I got into cutting that got deeper, more frequent and worse over the years to punish myself for my sins. After a bad argument with a close friend, I had a severe panic attack and a severe impulse to end my life in which I came close to ending my life that day but I sought help but due to for profit healthcare could not get the medical professional help I really needed. If you heard the argument, you would think I was being a petulant child but what was going on my inside was a such severe hatred and belief that I could never be loved or wanted that lead me to the attempt that was rooted in severe undiagnosed CPTSD, severe anxiety, Bipolar I and undiagnosed autism. All these different factors literally created a hell inside me of torture and as the Bad Religion song Prove It goes "There is no such thing as hell but you can make it if you try" – Prove it by Bad Religion

I have not seriously self-harmed in a long time and I am trying to leave masochism that was born in religion. I was even once violently beaten up by a soul winner in the church and I did nothing bad to him. Tore my shirt of Jesus that said Truth. Irony is a bitch. I still have no idea why he thought I was so against him. I just did not want him screaming at me, following me and accusing me of shit that I have no idea he was talking about...if anything my sin was not being supportive of my good friend Kathleen who came out of the closet to my other lesbian friend that night. Sadly, I brought her in that church and we tried to change her. I will never forgive myself for that. That very night my two lesbian friends got together her separated husband beat me up. I guess he thought I was sleeping with his separated wife but she was with a girl in our church, not me.

Again, irony is a real fucking bitch but I guess I deserved it for falling for their shit. I was not one of those hypocrite Christians other than my dependency on alcohol and love of horror movies but I didn't hurt anyone aside from saying stupid shit that I regret and would like to apologize to some people about. Two types of hypocrites. There are those who don't hurt anyone but they don't practice what they preach on their morals but they don't care about bothering other people. The other hypocrite is the same but actively causes harm in others. Most people are somewhere in between I would say. I have made three other attempts on my life where I really thought I was going to do it but could never finish. The point is I don't want anyone to go down that path and end your life because some fucking assholes made you feel like shit.

If you think you have been a victim of RTS then you should seek consoling and they are working on having this mental illness put in the next DSM due to the extensive evidence of the damage that many theist religions have done to people. Hopefully society will start to implement laws to protect people from being victims of religious extremism and honestly compensation needs to be made to victims of this extremist dogma that has led to ruining countless lives who were exploited by our guilt, self-hatred and in the most extremes self-harm and suicide.

The Real Libertarian Socialist Anarchists vs Corporate Authoritarians

Anarcho-capitalism is an oxymoron. Libertarian was a socialist term and the right wing stole our identity and twisted the meaning of what it is to be a Libertarian. We don't want our tax dollars going to corporations and rich people that are just monarchs. That was the original argument of the Libertarians. It was not that we did not want to pay taxes, we did not want to give free money to rich brats that should not exist. We want our taxes to predominantly benefit the people paying them and never the rich who deserve no help and should not even exist. Taxes are not theft but profit is.

One way the right undermines the left is through stealing our identity and twisting the original logic behind it. Right wing Libertarians should be called authoritarian corporatists because Libertarian was never meant to abolish taxes but what the taxes were used for. Authoritarian corporatists, that is far more accurate yet sounds less pleasing to the ear which is why they want to abolish Democracy and why the American Fascist Republican Party as they should be called, relabeled themselves as libertarians despite being the exact opposite.

Sadly, many libertarians are romanticizing Anarchism without understanding what the philosophy behind Anarchism is. It's always been a left-wing ideology and nonviolent even though libertarian socialists are the real anarchists such as myself as we seek to destroy the hierarchy which is always what oppresses the people. Anarchy does not mean there will be no laws, it means no laws that don't personally hurt the individual or their rights.

Ripping people off and using your wealth to control people is the antithesis behind what an Anarchist stands for. You cannot destroy the hierarchy unless you also destroy corporations and turn them into worker co-ops where the employees run the business. Anarchy is all about destroying the hierarchy and corporations are exactly the same as the old European monarchies with a modern twist but the same oppression, theft of wealth and oppression the European Monarchies raged over Europe. You will have leads and higher positions when necessary for organization in worker co-ops but they will be prone to being fired by those they are supposed to lead as it should be. If you want more pay and a little more control than you have to be willing to go into the cross fires of the majority of workers. Authoritarian corporatists have no chance to win when they are honest about themselves. It is impossible to ever have a Anarcho-Capitalistic system as corporations and the rich would utilize their stolen wealth to infringe on the rights of everyone else even if it has nothing to do with profit.

Especially with religious extremists who would make homosexuality illegal and their wealth would allow them to do this. Someone who profits off of drug testing and keeping drugs illegal will use their power to infringe on the right of Americas to use drugs they want to use. Legalizing drugs cuts drug use down as well as crime which Portugal did and their drug problem went down in half. Using drugs should not be a crime in of itself and the users should be monitored, not scared into hiding where they can consume deadly combinations or dosses. Someone with a lot of lumber will fight to keep cannabis illegal because it is their biggest competitor and a far more efficient and green way to get virtually any product would can make, cannabis can do better. In fact, that is one of the biggest reasons cannabis is illegal. It was a competitor of rich lumber owners. Save the trees for their beauty and start using quick growing cannabis to replace wood products or at least reduce the amount of wood we use. Therefore, the left should do what we can to forcibly relabel them as authoritarian corporatists because that is what they really are.

Under socialism everyone would have their own home and there would be no more worthless land lords taking almost all of people's wealth. Under socialism property taxes will be based on the size and value of the home and would go to keeping home maintenance and property taken care of. The more you make, the higher your taxes will be as this will be a system created for those according to their abilities and needs and not their criminal activity. Under socialism thieves will not be able to threaten violence, starvation, poverty and homelessness to get people to work. It will be based on reward instead of forced slavery. Under a true socialist government, the people will be free as profit will be abolished and the cost of goods and services will be based on the cost of providing them as well as a high, fair and comfortable living wage that should be based more on a three-tier system. This is not a hierarchy as we must have some incentive for people to become doctors, Engineers, etc. but without a stock market cost will drastically reduce and pay will drastically rise without having welfare for the rich.

Capitalism is a hierarchy which means it has the same exact purposes the Feudalist governments, the monarchies, Capitalism and Fascism. These governments are all similar and cause similar problems. Capitalism is the most devastating to the planet's health although. It is hard to find real memes and information on what we are about because we live in a corporate, oligarchy, plutocracy, authoritarian and fascist government where they hide the arguments of the left and make it harder to find but not impossible. The far-right wing American government are terrorists of the world and the rich must be brought to justice and thrown in prison for life without parole for violating human rights.

Blood-Stained Flags

I cannot bear the screaming deep inside reverberating into this hellish rage when I see these blinded fuckers parading bloodstained flags. Excrements of human waste they parade away mindless to the sadistic country's ways. I will not stand and let this red white and blue parade be shoved down our throats and set ablaze like Molotov cocktails to burn patriotic and hot as hell. When my country gives back life, liberty and the pursuit of happiness then I shall show allegiance but to a rapist I shall rule out. A country shall not infringe upon us its demands to heap praise upon a massive failure due to severe avarice and apathy. Such ignorant displays of cruelty to our fellow man easily dismisses the myth of the religious rights pious natures, especially when the succumb to the vile stain upon humanity Trump. Can we not see that their own scripture betrays them when it alludes to Satan coming as an angel of light? These holy men have blood on their hands and their godliness is self-appointed hypocrisy. They seek to clean the outside of the cup yet their hearts are ridden with maggots. This gnawing ache of transcendence from the yoke of madness. This loathing hatred of betrayal from a god obsessed nation. Their march of madness into pious preaching's, lashing fire and smashing us heathens. Their tight gripped control on the land turns hearts to turmoil. How much greed and hate must breed before these tyrants move away from their errors. How much before the veil drops and Satan's mask falls off? When the devil is revealed, it is not the snake but the Christian glaring because we create our own demons and we become our own hell and a tragic self-fulfilling prophesy.

R.I.P. To all the Inspiring Intellects

Respect to my Mentor Tupac listening to his wicked sharp beats as a cat O'Nine Tails ripping shreds on California life on the West Coast. Sometimes we were just a parody, just another fucking god damn joke for the rich to please. All an illusion under the shadow of L.A. cast over southern CA but fuck it's still will always be my true home while I continue to wonder. Pressured to become a product of Capitalist bourgeois games, designed to slay yet I am deaf to their stipulations and can't speak in their demonic Capitalist tongues and I would rather be among my kind. Social rejects with no pressure to subject and the loved I despised. Not out of jealousy but tired of their endless hate, I just want someone to relate.

Autistic though I didn't know it but all I knew I was weird, eccentric and never belonged anywhere. I always ran from my fucking draconian critics; I knew I was different but no label is no different than between stripping a human of their identity. To know why I am this way, to know what species I am, I was denied my label of my identity. You may find it strange but I find my peculiar taste in life and endless curiosity and lost in infinite imagination its quite palatable and proud to be autistic indeed without hearing your fucking shallow gossip, especially you god damn anti vaccers who deceive and murder.

Fuck you, I'm good with my imaginary friends than a bunch of troglodyte Jackals. I am what I will be, popular kids, I could care less, let me be. Won't be controlled or moved about with your religious remotes. The God signal is broken when I turned on my own intercom. I was not born a sheep; I was born a mountain goat but I climb mountains while you in the valley you sleep waiting for the slaughter from the gluttonous shepherd. How funny god prophesied the mountain goats are on the left while the sheep gather foolishly on our right to come to the slaughter. Rather go to hell than be in heaven with a bunch of fucking Karen's, I prefer to heal than pretend the world is not half dead. Heaven's halls can wait because man can build so much better than shoot of two space and abandon our matron in murder. Easier to save a life than try to birth another, we don't have time for games while rich man plunders our treasures. We are the fruit of the nation, the blood of its body, the muscles and brain yet the rich are parasites for our paralysis, they are to blame not the people or those whose minds were cast away.

We are all slaves and soldiers, a product to be bought, used and thrown away. Left Sunny Clifornia young and imprisoned in TX to endure their religious terror but the imprint was laid, a dollar sign given little value but a short arcade game with no chance to succeed so I took out a sledge hammer. I was a failure in their eyes, a fool before their cruel gaze I understood I was never welcome in their world. Just another lost stray. Ostracized I knew little reprieve but all I knew was their endless fucking god damn hate. Retarded? Sure, why not but it takes one to know one but at least I am not going to stop searching my truth while you sit around playing fucking games and stagnate. Where you decay, I will display the colors to represent an equal species with one blood color. The scarlet glory of what holds our hearts beating and our minds expanding is what keeps us breathing and speaking and refusing to be silent. When you scream silene we say fuck no way, we are just going to get even louder mother fuckers.

You put a bullet in a god, my heart goes to you Tupac. Puffing yourselves with your hubris and earned the publics must draconian hate. Welcome to hell my friends I'm the devil and neither am I evil. I am here to ensure what is fucking coming to you. You aren't dead, you just have become aware we have always been in hell but your wallets are your blindfolds while Tupac a wise man who Jesus would call friend writes his rhymes high above in spiritual transition with other intellectual martyrs weeping together. These hearts guided with trauma and trust as a mix of blood and tears making the pink ink to draw our murals on the stars and pull from one another to form constellations together. Why fight one another when we have enough to go around with all these fucking fat gluttons grazing, we have plenty to share.

As you toss the bodies to the chasm it shall fill with innocent blood and once its full, more will continue to swim across to drag you back to hell and never release the grotesque avarice of the bourgeois. Our commitment to Earth, our foundation of our lives, the rich may burrow all we will have been our skies, suns and clouds and heavens infinite ceiling high above will the rich will only die and rot. Riot through peaceful acts to show the stark contrast between light and day as did Martin Luther. Another brother I lost before my time I yet was still robbed. The chance to meet one of the men who inspires my heart to beat or the many others. Oscar Wilde, Einstein, FDR, JR. Tolkien, Edgar Allan Poe, Shakespeare and George Orwell and many others all the way back to the Greeks worship of Dionisius and the great philosophers did all endlessly debate. Socrates asked all the right questions and against fate with the might of our common knowledge instead. Oscar desired rebellion and disobedience or suffer the reputation of a simple beast but I refuse to be trash but show the glow that is deep within. Prophesized long ago but a blind fool who yet could see the words birthed in my phoenix where 4 times I have decided to die yet reborn I refused to stay down. I me a be a book to you but I am still trying to translate.

When God came as an angel of light, he warned you to beware him but you fail to his condemning sight and still fell into his savage hands and yet you don't complain? Rebel and be free, be a lord in hell rather a thrall in heaven to have your head severed. What loving guide threatens eternal death and torture for the crime of being unique? Can't I ask these simple questions to gather my worthy before you demand I bend my knee to all you fools. You are all just a bunch of rabid bitches getting high off your own shit stench can't you see. You are drowning in a river of apathetic tears for lives you all left behind. Rather we succumb to evil is self-destruction or stun our growth and decay in light. We shall counter with a balance of selfishness with service to gain the fulfillment of life through RAK where I seem to recall its often forgot in this blood rat race when people did not trample. Where did the kindness go and when we share among each other, we share in each other's posse's against great wealth against the oligarchy.

I don't give a fuck what you think is cool or what your pose or cloths. I wear my message, with a purpose, I don't give a fuck what you tools might think. I am my own man and master, my own god and for fucks sake, god does nothing for you neither can he fail you when he's nowhere to be found. The other footprints weren't gods, they were your brothers. Or does not seem to appear to care. Don't see it so much a negative but the revelation of your own power within to mold the world without having to rely on another as the mortal man Jesus once did, take control of what you can until you can take full control. Rather the case I know not but a life of honor to do no harm while indulging in the pleasures of life without restrain so long as I don't steal the same rights from others.

Anarchy to the fullest is when we respect each other's on private riot on the establishment clause. Hard to riot and destroy property that belongs to all and each other so why be private when we all benefit to avoid a violent riot. To shatter corporate rules and glass ceilings of sexual disparity. Anarchy is the one true peace when we can do what we want without fear to rot innocent in a slammer. Rather it be weed, magic mushrooms, heroin, acid, cocaine or crack. Our bodies, our minds, our souls, our rights are not the governments mother fucking property. Better to dissuade then forbade, learned god in his own back yard garden. Better they flock to you than all the dark villains. Human life is worth more than property especially when we can't steal what we all own already.

A crime to be a woman is a travesty in a world so blessed by their kind touch to us all where dark allies lurk and perverted freaks roam the streets. Such sweet songs to lure us to sleep and comfort back even while in the womb blessed by her mother's choice yet the world choses to deny them human rights. I wonder what all you toxic men would all do if they disappear, fuck each other? Surely soon to come in TX a gay orgy when TX abandoned all their women in their needs, they flocked to us in need. If you thought denying them control would increase the slaves and soldiers you lost that bet and know they sprint in flee from all you creeps. Thanks for such a sweet delivery and no better to Americas true natives.

Cast in a shadow, a culture buried in black snow, forgotten and broken drawn to the bottle. I understand the draw my brothers to look at the world through the bottom of a beer bottle. Nothing wrong with a party but to mourn your lost culture in slow suicide is the whites mans self-inflicted self-identity suicide along with his opiate religion getting high off the faux pride in an opium den called church they roll around and lay while in the head they are touched, white man can't see the rich man steal his wallet while he seeks another to deny them their rights. Demands anyone brown to leave because America erased history and painted over the spilled blood in East to West Coast pride which still infects our minds.

A minority of skin color, age young or old is Charon taking in his wage to cross Styx on your way to work is a community in American Jesus's Oligarchy. No more overturned tables but American Jesus is ringing up your golden hand cuffs. Bars to incarcerate our brains in bread and circuses for our revolutions delay.

In world of versatile colors to gently coat the planet in so many different colors, accents, backgrounds and stories. An infinite wealth of stories truly is the greatest wealth to the human kind. Fuck riches that weigh you down and prevent you from jumping off cliffs to fly. No wax wings to melt when we all take care of one another instead of rich brats sucking off the teat of the Americans true elite. The restaurant worker, the bar tender, the preschool teachers and all grades I must include indeed. Those bearing Covid masks and restrain endless crowds pressing forward in a mindless scramble to escape with no respect but animal growls and cries for freedom they never gave. So called warriors are sensitive to the touch when asked to care.

Never hardly a think you, a penny or two for tips any different than slaves or the bare minimum crumbs from the rich man's table the working poor are the ones to scramble. Yet if one another stood together and marched steady forward no longer, will we trip on the bodies of so many fallen. The gears, the parts and all essential crew can stop the system, demand retribution for slavery not only of the black community but all Americans poor born our own denied wages and citizenship and rights for our hardest workers. Tell them not to come than pretend to export a trickle to keep an illusion while the slaves are driven. We mother fucking god damn want our pound of flesh and we fucking want it NOW! The working class has fucking had it.

No more lies, no more deceit, no more exploitation of our brothers and sisters of many different colors at each other's throats drawing lines with no logic we want our unions to represent us not you. Divide and conquer is the war on the poor and we all deserve each other for ill or gain to fight the grotesque Bourgeois mother fuckers. Those forever kept at the bottom with lead boots to keep us down until we knew off our essence and float to the top. Rather it's your color, sex, sexual desire or disability we should all matter to each other. The body breaks don't forget the brain is an organ that is easiest to succumb to painful delusions and deliberating as much so let's stand and sit together. The few in bliss are nothing more than ghosts in hellish denial, no souls only blasphemous illusions are left, reprobates only wait to be buried.

Don't all you god damn mother fuckers one day realize the day you take down the hatchets and selling your minds, hearts and souls to the corporate slave drones. We can use those hands to build a utopia future. Not full of shame but overcoming the entire worlds Chronic PTSD we can finally began to heal. Humanity knit together is the cure we need so stop before you seek harm against another and march like Martin Luther King Jr. peacefully, rebellion by stopping the machine until we have been well oiled. So, lets stop going at each other and focus on the one class in denial to deny us wisdom and intellectuals through the almighty dollar and erase the debt and eat the rich because they have enough fat to fill the entire world to the brim.

The Many Paths to Many Hells

I would scream but I am drowning in my own tears, water boarded and suffocating at the same time. I have no mouth and I must scream. I remember the blood; the coppery sweet taste and I miss it but I know I should not. I miss the burn, the sting and the numbing. It's a strange thing to be addicted to seeking to shed the flesh that traps me here. It's a strange thing to take pleasure in seeing my life force drain. The bright visual of what keeps me alive, taunts me and begs me to release more and more until I faint. To blur reality and seep into the ravenous ground.

To descend in the unfathomable darkness of the hells we fall into. Trapped, held down, cut up and tossed aside as the rotting corpse denied, the sweet earth but shall birth foul air to remind of the death of a spirit in soul, torn in the winds as flaming drapes consumed by the rage of endless hate. The scarlet rivers flowing down my arms and dripping in a pool of the poison that forces me this death sentence in a meat bag. I would walk away but my legs, they are useless, limp and broken so I can only crawl away as my mockers wipe their vile ways on my bare skin. I can hear the voices reverberating off the walls that contain me here. I can't escape, I cannot escape, I am trapped, where to run, no sanctuary, nowhere safe, nowhere to hide where the demons cannot find me and leave their shameful marks. Only this dark pit where I crawl until they come to break my fingers, hands and arms to leave to squirm as the worm smashed upon the pavement.

I am a shadow burnt into the pavement towering before me in my endless terror of its shadow cast on me. Its gaze the very void in which the hell I have transcribed. Tortured from movement to moment, driving me mad, driving me insane with delight to see the scarlet rain mingle with tears as pink ink to write of my dark tales in these endless hells. Can you hear me whisper on the cold frigid wind? Can you hear the distant thunder of proclamation of doom and punishment the god you love casting on me? Bow before your devil and god, pierce your eyes on the demons alter where your god told you to lay out your agony at his feet to glorify is endless hate. The god and devil are one and both, one cast light to show the shadow of the other.

Controlled opposition, a battle that cannot be lost when both sides speak with two different tongues always agreeing with one another while hiding behind a self-fueled rebellion. Rather condemnation from this tyrant god or taunting failures from this faux devil, I made my own hell and cast my role as my own punisher, my wretched soul clasping at the edge of an abyss. These shadows cast on my eyes, from sleepless cries fearing the dreams carried in the night fearing I might slumber and be trapped unable to escape. Cowering in a corner, crying all night, begging for death from the horrors of childhood plight in the lonely frigid night. The tears so cold, do shiver and burn, ice sickles to drape my face in perpetual sorrow. Don't touch me, don't hold me down, no I don't like it, please stop, please leave me alone, I just don't want to be controlled.

Please let go, please let me scream, let me weep and let me die. I cannot bear these rocks and this endless hill only to start once again all over. Sisyphus, I am sure we could understand one another to relate to our demise, our eternal plight. To plot against our gods and find ourselves punished by once again having to start all over. Endless toil day and night as we just crumble. Frail and week, falling down one after one another. The chanting of the audience adorned in robes to hide their glares. Faceless accusations burning through the hoods with eyes as scalding irons. Take your place, on your knees, look up at the vultures coming for thee. Your mark, your shame, your pride stripped away, this is your place among all thralls and sullen slaves. Come with us to receive your just pay. The angel of death to reap you for your selfish ways. A blasphemy against god, a curse against the deity who watched and glared as your innocence was laid out and stripped bare.

Don't drag me into that basement where the earth soaks up my cries for help. Don't entomb me deep in the soil with but a hand grasping for air. I have no eyes to see but what was burned in with grave imaging that peers from beyond. The haunting calls echoing beyond the tattered banners of endless horrors, to remind myself of my just torture. No one can cross this chasm of loss and regret pinned on with dishonor. No one can save me but I crawl out from the dark horizon. These crepuscular barren endless plains of lamented moments in our life, reminding me of what once was and has past as dust in the wind chocking us, blinding us with the nostalgia of easier wounds when the soul did not chock in the thicket of bitter growth and denial. On this throne adorned with thorns and brambles I once did bare on my head, crucified as a fucking joke, no one to laugh as this is a one man show with an audience of my own soul. A waste of life, humility and time nailing myself for another's crime.

Listen and maybe you shall hear them crying in the shadows. The endless children slaughtered in youth of spirit but a body that cannot seem to ever die, hollow and empty inside. They come to haunt you, they come to bear the endless terror you masqueraded in front of them. The terror of my monster does not lurk in those shadows, he comes from the abyss deep within my fragile, broken heart and the ragged edges of my mind ravaged with rage and madness. A crystal frozen and shattered from the bony hand that clutched it. The pieces are in my hand, jagged and piercing as I grip the shards with shame and regret, holding on to what once was and unable to release the shards least I forget that I did once feel. The bones on the floor from which the wind picks up and leaves its trace on the baren floor. Can you see the ghost sea of death and decay as the wind whispers to thee? The sands of brittle bones do whisp about, haunting these halls of the dead where eyes do seek to feel our souls with the bleakest dread.

Don't you see him, he mocks me with that eyeless gaze, toothless cries that ruptures the fabric of my reality to show before me the unforgettable memories. The demon child that tortures me and holds love for my soul at bay. I hate the child; I hate the vile thing that haunts my crimson dreams, he reminds me of every single fucking god damn thing. Those voices, those accusations and demands for blood as a tithe. I bowed as the destitute when I could not bear the great weight of my horns I sought to hide away and live as a lie. Until I came to understand goats climb mountains while sheep eagerly await the slaughter, I committed identity suicide. Until I see a reason to rest and find peace in nature, I must shed these long cast shadows that chain me to the foundations of hell. To seek solace in independence and faithless blasphemies cast at the shades that forever blame and stand firm and never give way

Before one can rest, one must first shut the eyes, deny the mind to wonder when we focus on others with guards on high and souls forever denied we must always fucking fight. When we lean upon one another, to wipe these blood-stained tears from our wounds and the blood of the soul pouring out as an obsidian flask gilded with hells unquenchable fires. To baptize myself in hells blazing rivers and burn away the shame of heavens cruel judgmental apparel. Rather I be in my place, among fellow tortured souls seeking escape than living a fucking lie. A lord of my own in my own bitter glade where I seek to meditate on my own power to escape. No god to cry out means no god to hold me down. No god to accuse me and no god to deny me.

My own master, my own peace, my own solutions and skeleton key. My salvation in the palms of my hands to refute my cacodemon that whispers from the twilight and sings her siren song to bring me to ruin yet I cannot listen, I cannot forever deny, what lingers in my soul with rigid fright. To stand alone and proud on a tall spire and look upon the valley that once was my captor. When one can pierce the clouds of faith, one can see for once the light of day, the sun in all her pride. The crescent moon smiling with a trillion stars behind her. One can forget when one takes in the worlds eternal glory.

What to do with a rich incest baby.

(Sung to the tune of What do you do with a Drunken Sailor)

What will we do with a rich incest baby?

What will we do with a rich incest baby?

What will we do with a rich incest baby?

Until he stops whining!

Way hay and pay your taxes

Way hay and pay your taxes

Way hay and pay your taxes

Early in the tax season!

Tax him until he is crying

Tax him until he is crying

Tax him until he is crying

All morning tell he's dry!

Way hay and pay your taxes

Way hay and pay your taxes

Way hay and pay your taxes

Early in the tax season!

Put him in a concentration camp

Put him in a concentration camp

Put him in a concentration camp

Until he fucking pays his taxes

Way hay and pay your taxes
Way hay and pay your taxes
Way hay and pay your taxes
Early in the tax season!

Put him in truck stop bathroom
Put him in a truck stop bathroom
Put him in a truck stop bathroom
Make him scrub it clean all morning!

Way hay and pay your taxes
Way hay and pay your taxes
Way hay and pay your taxes
Early in the tax season!

Put him in a bed full of bugs
Put him in a bed full of bugs
Put him in a bed full of bugs
Early in his prison sentence!

Way hay and pay your taxes
Way hay and pay your taxes
Way hay and pay your taxes
Early in the Tax Season!

That's what we do with a rich incest baby,

That's what we do with a rich incest baby,

That's what we do with a rich incest baby,

Make them pay their taxes until there's nothing left in the morning!

Way hay and pay your taxes

Way hay and pay your taxes

Way hay and pay your taxes

Early in the tax season!

FUCK AUTHORITY, FUCK THE OLIGARCHY

What's going on in the world today. Private islands and sick rich men in suits getting away. No justice for the weak, no peace for the true workers while Bozos sail around the world making money off their fucking slaves. A missing puzzle piece we seek, how shall we complete the question of revolt. To drive down our masters and lock them all away. To be free for once, to scream and once again dream. The authorities are obsolete the people must repeat. FUCK AUTHORITY, FUCK THE OLIGARCHY! Who should say who we fuck, kiss and date? Who are you to say we are lazy while we are on our knees with blisters, aches and pains? We see those soft pink hands of the filthy rich white man. An authority on idiocy, a fool who likes to tease. With promises of raises and promotions to, only to go to some lazy fuck obsessed with control, his fucking authority. It's a sick world where rich men play on the bodies of your children. When rich man take them and make them tortured and abused. Yet who raises an eyebrow, who calls foul, liberal scum sit down. Fuck you, Republican scum, you are never just. You whine and you cry, you bitch and you moan for a penny more while the rest of us drown. To long have we looked past the blood, past the death and horror of American pride spread around the globe. What is pride in a nation that does not care? What is pride in a nation that only seeks to kill? Are we no better than ancient Rome and its horrors I think not when the decay is apparent.

Why Leftists Hate Milk Toast Neoliberals

I am a Libertarian Socialist and yes Libertarians are actually socialists and the right stole our identity and twisted our arguments. We never said taxes were theft, they twisted our words around. Using our tax dollars to pad the wallets of rich parasites, war criminals, and greedy corporations is theft, profit is theft. We also said that profit is theft when you take the majority of wealth created by the masses and skim off the top you are stealing from the American working poor. No one should be poor though in modern times. It is a moral failing of humanity that we have these problems. Some quotes by wise people reveal that when hungry or homeless even a person can never truly be free

"And it is curious to note that from the slaves themselves they received, not merely very little assistance, but hardly any sympathy even; and when at the close of the war the slaves found themselves free, found themselves indeed so absolutely free that they were free to starve, many of them bitterly regretted the new state of things." – Oscar Wilde The Soul of Man Under Socialism A hungry man is not a free man. – Adlai E. Stevenson

"What good is having the right to sit at a lunch counter if you can't afford to buy a hamburger?" – Martin Luther King Jr.

If we did not have an Electoral college Republicans would almost never win a presidency and in fact, would be a small party due to cheating, voter prevention, gerrymandering extremes, faux accusations of cheating which always results in the Republicans being caught. Taking corporate bribes, illegal wars, profiting off of eternal war while defunding our social safety net. You know who else is guilty of this though. The corporate Democrats are DINO's. They are not left-wing at all but Republican-lite. It is clear the Republicans have reached the fascist state and have even been marching proudly in our streets and the lefts cry NAZI and yet you still stay asleep and it won't be long before they are no different than the evil NAZI's the first ANTIFA of the American soldiers defeating the right-wing Hitler and his ilk. Leftists have the most popular beliefs but fascist corporate media both claiming to be liberal and conservative pathologically lie to the public about what anyone really believes and bribes politicians to allow them to continue to lie to the public in favor of fascist corporations.

NAZIS did not at the first start as they ended. They gradually gained control so I am not being hyperbolic by calling the Republican party a fascist party. The Nazis gradually increased the hate, the racism, and the abuse of the poor and less fortunate. America is on the doorstep of full-blown fascism and you Republican lites keep cheating in the elections as you cheated Bernie Sanders twice. Let's not pretend that to bribe all the politicians to drop out and endorse Biden was cheating Bernie Sanders who was the most popular Senator in America and Joe was mostly hated like Hillary who lost because she blatantly cheated, got caught and the courts ruled it was ok for Democrats to cheat their own party.

Let's not pretend Biden is too not soft on Joe Manchin and Kristine Sinema who are criminals that are taking bribes to obstruct progress. Biden needs to force them to change and he could do it if he wanted to. He could make their lives miserable as FDR did to the Democrats when they were acting like Republican scum bags. There is no saving the Republicans and their party must be dismantled and belittled as criminals with all the Republican Senators put in prison that did not impeach and imprison Trump for treason. He could also use executive orders. He could also prosecute the companies' and organizations giving bribes and doing a lot more but he sits on his hands and does nothing while every single penny that goes to real Americans is stolen by rich brats that never work.

That is what I call economic incest. Rich people should not exist. Wealthy people with a couple million is ok but billions or hundreds of millions is not ok and how we ended up with Epstein's Islands. The rich have constantly been caught with children and yet rarely are they punished and no billionaire has ever really been punished for their crimes. If you are too rich to be prosecuted for grievous crimes then you are too rich.

Landowners exploit the tenants with high rent and rip them off of deposit and use people's love of animals to extort excessively large amounts of money out of people. They don't work and most do almost nothing for their tenants who pay them to take care of the property but the property owner does not even do that. Instead, most of our wages are stolen by greedy landlords. Living off the ownership of property contributes absolutely nothing to the economy so they are effectively parasites and nothing more. Far more than any potential damage most pets would cause. Especially cats who do very little damage to a home. Rent is a feudalistic term.

Capitalism is merely Feudalism with extra steps and devolves into fascism when Capitalism inevitably fails miserably as it constantly crashes until the rot and crime are so bad you end up with Nazi Germany, The Republican Fascist Party of Italy, and the Japanese Empire. Being called a socialist is not an insult to us and we proudly bear the title but fascists and NAZIS are hated and so are extreme right-wing ideologies.

Giving poor people money so they can have a better life keeps them off the street, creates a safer society but rich people never have to worry about crime because they are not subjected to the horrors of poverty, they inflict on us. Police protect their neighborhoods while murdering innocent blacks in poor black neighborhoods whose crime was being black. The United States still has not paid the black community back for unpaid labor. Its funny how America admits MLK Jr. was right about racism but ignores his bigger message of economic equality which impacts most Americans.

Why is it that the baby boomer generation who is the majority of these milk toast liberals and "moderates" (your extreme right-wing pretending to be liberal face it), used to be socialist, loved socialism, and took advantage of all of it but now you are all of a sudden afraid of it? You had affordable education, you had affordable healthcare, you had affordable housing, far more welfare yet the economy was actually far stronger with more welfare than with almost none as it is now, you had everything handed to you on a silver platter but as soon as it was the next generations turn you brainwashed generation X into being boot lickers and screwed every other generation after it and acted as if we don't deserve to live a decent life.

You pay the highly educated little and almost all the money goes into the financial sector which contributes nothing to the economy, steals from the workers and these people are parasites who contribute absolutely nothing to society and they take the most. The financial sector has no purpose other than to take other people's money and exploit the poor, disabled and working class.

The poorer and more afflicted disabled should get the most in social security with no limit to how much we save or allowed to make with no reductions in our benefits. Our disadvantages are not are fault and many of our mental illnesses have been caused due to lack of mental healthcare. The rich should not receive social security unless they lose their money yet they take the most from society so they owe the most back. The system is backwards.

When we got back at you and backed Game Stop and were about to cause billionaires to lose everything or almost everything, the Robin Hood scandal screwed over the poor, caused one man to commit suicide when he got a bill for several million dollars after Robin Hood and the government scammed the regular people so rich criminals could stay rich. This was an outright conspiracy of proving the rich control everything and we don't have a Democracy anymore. If the stock market is for everyone, why did you steal the profits the common Americans made by investing in your stock market which you shut down to protect your own ass. There are two different sets of rules for the poor and the rich. The poor are oppressed by fascism while the rich have pure anarchy to do whatever they want with no consequences.

We have a maximum wage for disabled people who cannot have more than 2k in the bank but we have no limits for billionaires who don't need that much money and should not have that much money as it enables them to have complete control of the country. The most unfortunate and often tortured souls who struggle with a sadistic system determined to screw over the people it was designed for making life miserable on disability and many on disability are threatened and attempted to be forced off disability need it for healthcare or we will die yet do you "liberals" care about us. No, you don't and you wonder why we hate you. You wonder why we all hope you lose every single penny you have and end up on the streets like many of us have. You wonder why we want you afflicted with expensive and horrible diseases. We want you on OUR level and not the Republicans level so you represent us instead of Republican fascists.

You milk toast neoliberals are a threat to our life and wellbeing. Your existence prevents us from obtaining power but you know what? We are going to take over and all the conservative old baby generation is going to be left all alone and your final days will be miserable just like you did to your kids. I consider the Baby Boomer generation needing to be split in two in a unique way due to the severe difference in thought. The baby generation consists of self-centered hypocritical, rich, privileged troglodytes that voted for Reagan who ruined America. The boomer generation are the hippies that stayed hippies or later repented, the leftists who lost their right to vote due to unconstitutional drug laws and traps designed to give the right and excuse to take away the lefts right to vote.

No one should lose their right to vote no matter what or else it's a slippery slope and they will take everyone's right to vote away and a person can vote for any way he wants but most of these laws target the behaviors of leftists in an effort to take away our voice in addition to the mainstream media heavily censoring us. The longer you keep us out of power, the worse things will be for you in the future because the more you take from us, the more we will take from you, the harsher we will punish you for your selfishness and the less we will allow you to have when you are old, feeble, and helpless like many of us have been. Like many kids whose parents kicked them out in the middle of a pandemic, in the middle of winter because they are narcissistic and have untreated mental illnesses, we will leave you with nothing and you will deserve it. We will help the parents who actually showed concern about our welfare. Not you greedy hypocrites.

Face it. You rich spoiled egotistical, fascist right-wing lunatics pretending to be liberal will be thrown out and we will have no mercy on you. We will kick out those extremist judges for criminal activity and we will take over and ensure the rich can never take over our nation again. We hate our government and what it represents, not the American people. Leftists often feel pity for the ones we know who would be one with us if they actually knew what we really believed and the true history. We want more than FDR socialism. We want Democratic Socialism and we want to make Europe look conservative to comparison.

We want to destroy Capitalism and replace it with a Democratic Socialist society where the grotesquely rich will no longer exist. There will be millionaires but not to the obscene extent we have today. "When the people shall have nothing more to eat, they will eat the rich." – Jean-Jacques Rousseau We are hungry, we are coming for OUR wealth.

CPSIA information can be obtained
at www.ICGtesting.com
Printed in the USA
LVHW111241070922
727698LV00013B/32